colourful gardening

roses

colourful gardening

roses

Richard Ross

with photography by **Jerry Harpur** and **Marcus Harpur**

RYLAND
PETERS
& SMALL

Senior designer	Ashley Western
Designers	Sailesh Patel, Peter Jackson
Senior editor	Annabel Morgan
Editor	Jane Chapman
Picture research	Mel Watson, Kate Brunt
Production controller	Patricia Harrington
Publishing director	Anne Ryland

First published in Great Britain in 1999
by Ryland Peters & Small
Cavendish House
51–55 Mortimer Street
London W1N 7TD

ISBN 1 900518 79 1

A catalogue record for this book is available
from the British Library.

Printed and bound in China by Toppan Printing Co.
10 9 8 7 6 5 4 3 2 1

contents

Introduction   6

Rose classification   10

Species roses   12

Old garden roses   22

Modern shrub roses   32

Large-flowered roses   42

Cluster-flowered roses   50

Climbers and Ramblers   58

Miniature and Patio roses   68

Care and cultivation   74

Index   78

Plant index   78

Picture credits   80

Introduction

Roses have been around for a long time. A fossilized rose leaf has been found that is estimated to be 35 million years old. The first recorded painting of a rose is dated to approximately 2,000 BC in Crete. The first double rose was recorded in 470 BC. Gallica roses were grown by the Greeks and Romans. A 1st-century governor of Sicily was famous for holding a bag of roses to his nose whenever he had to meet the riff-raff, to disguise their less-than-sweet smell. The Roman Emperor Nero showered his dinner guests in rose petals. As early as the 13th century, rose fields at Provins, near Paris, were mass growing the Apothecary's rose, popular because its delicious perfume did not fade even when the flower was dried and powdered. Rose fields then, as now, were big business.

A sudden expansion of red roses took place in the 17th and 18th centuries, thanks to the tireless endeavours of Dutch rose breeders. As a result, about a dozen cultivated varieties increased to approximately 1,000. Roses became increasingly popular and sought-after. The great rose garden at Malmaison, near Paris, created by the Empress Josephine (1763–1814) and estimated to be the biggest rose collection at that time, made rose growing chic and brought a competitive edge to the pastime.

The biggest breakthrough in rose breeding came with the introduction of the repeat-flowering China roses to Europe and America in the late 18th century. The impact of the Chinas was huge. Tea clippers returning from China brought a cargo of Tea

Far left top: **The graceful, rose-pink Bourbon 'Reine Victoria' combines Old rose good looks and fragrance with a long flowering period.**

Far left bottom: **Roses join forces with hops, achilleas, monardas, hemerocallis and bergenias to produce this lively display.**

Left top: **Clematis and roses are perfect companions. Here** is *R.* × odorata 'Mutabilis' with the light blue *Clematis* 'Countess of Lovelace'.

Below: **The Hybrid Musk 'Buff Beauty' will help to form a dense hedge of large, rich apricot-yellow blooms.**

Below left: **The Cluster-flowered 'Jacqueline du Pré', with sweetly scented blush-pink flowers, is perfect for the front of the border.**

and China roses in their holds. European growers began to experiment with these exciting new forms, leading to the development of the Bourbon rose – a natural cross between a Damask and a China – and the Noisettes, a cross between a China and a Musk. These experiments led to roses that could flower for longer, and also made available a range of brighter, bolder colours. Nearly as great a breakthrough in rose breeding occurred earlier in the 20th century, when *R. foetida* 'Persiana' made bright yellow roses available for the first time.

Six hundred years on, and roses now represent big money if you can raise a winner. But rose breeding is a lottery – the occasional big win hides hundreds of losses. A large commercial rose breeder might have 100,000 seedling roses on trial at this moment, each one slightly different to all the others as well as to all the existing roses. Out of all these seedlings, perhaps ten will pass the marketability tests and actually end up in garden centres. These tests include good colour, shape, scent, repeat flowering, novelty value and, especially, disease resistance, as gardeners become better informed about ecological concerns and more reluctant to use pesticides. The whole process of creating a new rose can take ten years or longer.

Modern rose breeders have made enormous strides in rose technology, resulting in ever more disease-resistant plants that combine a good habit with beautiful flowers and delicious scent. Roses are now available in a spectrum of colours. However, true blue is still not available, although genetic breeding may yet crack that one, nor is true black, although the deepest purply-red roses burn badly in the sun, turning them black around the edges. The latest advances have resulted in the 1.8–3 m (6–10 ft) high climbers, which flower all summer, as well as miniature climbers with 5 cm (2 in) wide flowers – ideal if you have a small garden.

Roses are evolving fast. What will they look like by the end of the 22nd century? Bigger, brighter, and highly scented, no doubt. Disease resistance will probably be the norm. Some roses may even glow in the dark. Work has already begun using the gene that makes jellyfish luminous. The resulting roses glow when they are stressed, and the flash of light is picked up by distant satellites. Farmers are bleeped and rush to their growing fields to check that all is well. Using that gene, or alternatively one from a firefly, may result in roses that glow when patted, ruffled or stroked. Forget colour – the rose for the next century may be one that really does light up the border.

Roses are now available in a spectrum of colours. However, true blue is still not available, although genetic breeding may yet crack that one.

Right: **Roses burst through the smooth columns of yew (*Taxus*) in a garden that** **juxtaposes different shapes and combines the formal with the informal.**

Rose classification

Roses can be divided into three main groups: the Species roses, the Old garden roses, and the Modern garden roses. The Species roses include some shrubs and some climbers. They generally produce delicate, single flowers with five petals, many scented, that appear in early summer on second-year-old stems, followed by masses of colourful red hips. Some are absolute monsters – *Rosa filipes* 'Kiftsgate' spreads 15 x 30 m (50 x 100 ft), for example, and will easily clamber all over a tree. With all the broo-ha-ha about new roses, the Species roses are often overlooked, and you may have to purchase them at a specialist nursery. But it is well worth tracking them down – there are some with terrific and unusual detail, such as the 2.5 m (8 ft) high *Rosa sericea pteracantha,* which has bizarre and beautiful stems. The large thorns are bright red and translucent, wide, flat and triangular. Forget about the flowers – trail the stems so the sun can illuminate the thorns.

The Old garden roses consist of 11 different groups (the Noisettes are Old garden roses but are grouped with Climbers). Many people believe that Old garden roses flower only once, but don't be misled. Roughly half of the rose groups in this category are remontant – that is, they repeat flower throughout the season – and many have the added bonus of a big fruity scent. They are excellent for hedges (Gallicas), shade (Albas), scent ('Mme Isaac Pereire'), old-fashioned cottage gardens (Moss roses) and big, plump roses that bend a stem right over ('Marie Louise').

I have divided the Modern roses into five groups. The first group consists of the Modern shrub roses, a very diverse group that includes the English roses – the most important group of the late 20th century – which combine wonderful Old rose looks and scent, with modern repeat flowering, and popular Shrub roses such as 'Fritz Nobis', which has a spicy scent and orange-red hips. This group also contains Ground-cover roses ('Max Graf'), which do not really pack the ground with dense layers blocking out weeds, but can put on an incredibly

impressive display, forming a thick blanket of blooms. It also includes the Hybrid Musks, which produce great massed sprays of flowers. And the Rugosas are equally good as individual eye-catchers or hedges with good flowers, scent and hips.

The second group of Modern roses are the Hybrid Teas, now known as Large-flowered bush roses. They guarantee a good show all summer and produce large, conical flowers, often double, with luscious looks and plenty of scent. This group includes old favourites like 'Peace' and new entries like 'Warm Wishes', which has piled up a stack of awards. The emphasis is on individual flowers rather than the plant as a whole. The third group is the Cluster-flowered bush roses, or Floribundas, which are amazingly useful plants, providing a massed supply of smaller flowers all summer long. Next come the Climbers and Ramblers. The former include a good range of repeat-flowering cultivars, many of which are also highly scented. The Ramblers are highly vigorous. They produce smaller, numerous flowers in big clusters, appearing once a year, on stiffer stems with glossy leaves. The

final group is the Miniature and Patio roses. It includes Miniatures, 30 cm (12 in) high, now back in fashion, Patio roses which are 15 cm (6 in) taller, and the new Climbing Small Miniatures, which are 2.2–2.7 m (7–9 ft) high.

Although some books on roses devote a separate section to standard roses, they are not actually a specific group. In fact, roses from several different groups can be grown as standards. This way of growing roses – as miniature trees on an elongated stem – first came into vogue about 100 years ago. There are two different types. The weeping standards tumble and spray outwards, while the rest have a largish ball of flowers and foliage on top of a long thin stem. Standards are usually bought ready-trained and can be used in many different and imaginative ways: marking the corners of a square pond; as the centrepiece in an island bed; lining both sides of a path like a string of sentries standing to attention; or behind a narrow box edging in a small formal garden. Heights vary. Some nurseries offer, say, five ranges between 45 cm (18 in) and 1.5 m (5 ft).

Above left: **Some rose gardens can look rigid and uniformly posed. Not this rose bed in a Paris park. Mixed colours and dramatic verticals show how wonderful roses can be when grown** *en masse.*

Above: **The exquisite, rich pink, scented blooms of the English rose 'Gertrude Jekyll' are offset by the pinks and whites of the petunias and nicotianas.**

Far left: **Pelargoniums and spider plants make highly effective rose companions.**

Species roses are the wild ancestors of the familiar garden rose. They come in many different shapes and sizes, but are mostly large shrubs or climbers that flower once yearly, producing single flowers in spring or summer, followed by decoratively shaped, colourful hips in autumn.

species roses

There are at least 140 wild species found growing in the northern hemisphere; most are hardy and originate from the Far East. Species roses are quite different to the well-mannered, upright, repeat-flowering, large-flowered roses found in a neatly manicured border or formal rose garden. They are usually large shrubs or climbers with long, arching shoots that bear simple, mainly single, flowers, often sweetly scented. They generally have only one flush of flowers, in early to mid-summer. In addition, many species roses have attractive boldly coloured hips following on from the flowers.

Species roses come in many different shapes and sizes. They include some fabulous giants and some tiny gems. They vary from the intense rich red, 3.7 m (12 ft) high *Rosa* 'Geranium', a *moyesii* hybrid, one of the best species, with 8 cm (3 in) wide flowers and striking flagon-shaped crimson hips, to *R. rugosa*, which forms wonderful great thickets and hedges and even grows on sandy beaches in Japan, to the prostrate *R. wichurana*, which provides 6 m (20 ft) of ground cover. Species roses have many virtues – they can be very vigorous, virtually disease resistant and require hardly any pruning, just a quick tidy after flowering.

Climbers and ramblers

Species climbers produce clusters of single flowers appearing on last year's growth, some with a terrific scent. *Rosa filipes* 'Kiftsgate' is the biggest. This is a beautiful giant – allow for it to grow as high as 15 m (50 ft), and up to 30 m (100 ft) in width. It needs at least two trees to shoot over, and will cover them with a shower of creamy-white flowers in mid-summer. Planted at the back of a garden, it also offers first-rate security – any intruder would have to be extremely determined to clamber through such a thorny thicket. The only drawback to growing *R. f.* 'Kiftsgate' is the fact that it can be slow to take off. Impatient rose lovers

Left top: **A fun way to grow *R. filipes* 'Kiftsgate' is in a walled garden, where the enclosed space quickly fills up with the fruity scent.**

Left bottom: **A sturdy, open tree provides the perfect frame for a climbing rose. Here a tall tree plays host to the twining, creamy-white flowers of *Rosa helenae*.**

Far left: **The vigorous *R. wichurana,* which has parented many excellent ramblers, is equally good going up as making dense, trailing ground cover.**

should try instead the vigorous *R. mulliganii,* which is covered with small white flowers and glossy dark green leaves. It is a fast grower, issuing new shoots that can grow as much as 5.5 m (18 ft) in a summer. *R. mulliganii* has a mature height in the region of 6–7.5 m (20–25 ft), and generally spreads to about 4.5 m (15 ft).

R. brunonii, the Himalayan Musk, is another giant that can hit 7.5 x 4.5 m (25 x 15 ft), its vicious thorns combined with creamy-white flowers. *R. b.* 'La Mortola' can grow slightly higher, with double the spread, and many consider it superior. Both are slightly tender, needing a sheltered corner of a warm garden. *R. rubus* is an unusual species rose because it flowers from early to late summer, also reaching 7.5 m (25 ft), with tight clusters of creamy-white flowers. Both of these look wonderful covering a copper beech, their long flowering stems trailing down.

If you have a small garden, try one of the excellent medium-sized species climbers, which will add a picturesque element to any corner of the garden, clambering round old apple trees, or scrambling over hedges. *R. helenae* is perhaps the pick of the bunch. It grows to 6 m (20 ft) and has the creamy-white flowers so typical of species roses, standing out in clusters against the dark green leaves. There is a good show of orangey-red hips, but beware the vicious thorns. *R. multiflora* carries large clusters of cupped white flowers and makes tough dense growth. Reaching 2.2 m (7 ft) high, it can form an impenetrable hedge and doubles up as a windbreak. If it is allowed to scramble up and around the trunk and branches of a tree, it can reach 6 m (20 ft).

Rosa wichurana is equally remarkable. This vigorous rose does not begin flowering until late summer, when the other species have finished. It is almost evergreen, with glossy dark green leaves, white flowers and golden stamens. A rose of many

Species roses are the wild rose ancestors of the familiar garden rose. At least 140 species roses have been found growing in the wild.

talents, *R. wichurana* can be sent up a pergola or trained across a brick wall. It can even be used as ground cover – the prostrate growth can spread 4.5–6 m (15–20 ft), making a good background for whites, yellows and reds.

The shortest species climbers are in the 3–4.5 m (10–15 ft) high range. *R. moschata* carries clusters of fragile-looking creamy-white flowers against a dramatic backdrop of purplish-green leaves. Like *R. wichurana*, it does not flower until late summer. And *R. longicuspis* var. *sinowilsonii*, which flowers in early summer, deserves to be called a climber because it can grow 9 m (30 ft) high, but it tends to get cut back by frosts when not grown against warm, sheltered, south-facing walls, ending up half that height. What makes it special are the fabulous leaves, dark green above, and shiny beneath, tinted purple-brown.

There are very few species ramblers, but the best are the Banksian roses. *R. banksiae* var. *banksiae* is stupendous. It grows as tall as 9 m (30 ft), can easily cover a tree, and produces thousands of small, white, deliciously scented flowers on virtually thornless stems in late spring and early summer. It needs a warm site in a mild region. There are only a couple of drawbacks – it can take a couple of years to flower, like all Banksians, and it is susceptible to frosts. *R. banksiae* 'Lutea' is a yellow version that is extremely pretty, but does not possess the powerful scent.

Shrubs

One of the best, most exciting and unusual species roses is the shrubby *R. sericea* subsp. *omeiensis* f. *pteracantha*. Each stem is studded with fabulous translucent wine-red thorns, 2 cm (³/₄ in) wide at the base, and startlingly reminiscent of the ridged spine of a prehistoric monster. The white flowers are pretty, but cannot compete with the striking thorns. Grow this 2.5 m (8 ft) high shrub where the sun can illuminate the thorns from behind. It makes a novel hedge. The disease-free, tough and hardy *Rosa rugosa* makes an equally good hedge, and grows particularly well in sandy soils by the sea. It grows up to 2.2 x 2.2 m (7 x 7 ft), so you do not need to plant many to create a dense barrier. The purple-rose single flowers start opening in early summer, followed by bright orange-red hips. By growing *R. r.* 'Alba', you will enjoy a two-tone display of white flowers and red hips. *R. forrestiana* will also make a fine hedge, about 1.8 m (6 ft) high. It combines bright green foliage with abundant crimson flowers, followed by bright red hips held, like nuts, in green bracts.

For the best species hedge, use a mix of different roses; any will do provided they are tall, bushy and vigorous, like the pink *R. virginiana*, 1.5 m (5 ft) high, which flowers all summer and thrives on sandy soils, its decorative hips persisting through the winter. In addition, the foliage takes on vibrant autumnal tints. *R. eglanteria*, the sweet briar, has the added bonus of scented leaves that are particularly pungent on warm, damp days. Growing to a height of 2.2 m (7 ft), with plenty of prickles, it makes an impenetrable barrier, but is extremely pretty at the same time, with delicate pink petals, golden stamens and hips lasting into winter. *R. villosa* is another stunner that will form a good hedge. It grows to a height of 3 m (10 ft) and is covered with pink flowers followed by rich red hips.

If you have space for a taller species rose in your border, perhaps grown as a specimen plant, *R. glauca* is a must. It stands 2.5 m (8 ft) high, like a young, spare, beautiful tree, with copper-

Far left: **The vigorous *R. banksiae* var. *banksiae* needs a warm, sheltered, sunny garden to thrive.**

Left: **Grow *R. glauca* close to a path where it can be clearly seen and appreciated. This rose's chief value is its stiff vertical growth, which can be pruned and opened up, its glaucous leaves and tinted stems. A definite 'must', even without the mass of pink flowers.**

Below: **'Fru Dagmar Hastrup' is a Rugosa rose with pink flowers followed by crimson hips. It makes a fine, 1.5 m (5 ft) high hedge.**

R. glauca is a must. It is like a young, spare, beautiful tree, with copper-red stems.

red new stems, striking slate-blue foliage and pale pink flowers with a white centre. Clusters of red hips follow the flowers in autumn. *R.* 'Geranium' (a *moyesii* hybrid) is perhaps the best and most beautiful species rose. The satiny flowers are rich deep red but scentless. However, this rose is worth growing for the hips alone – appearing in late summer, they resemble miniature orange-red flasks. The 3.7 m (12 ft) high gaunt growth is ideal for the back of the border. Do not plant either of these beauties anywhere near *R. macrophylla*, which is an eye-catching monster that can reach 4.3 m (14 ft) high and wide and overpowers everything around it.

Other outstanding shrub species include *R. webbiana*, *R. multibracteata* and *R. willmottiae*, three roses with delicate pink flowers, all about 1.8 m (6 ft) high. On a smaller scale, *R. pimpinellifolia* grows in mounds 90 cm (3 ft) high. It has an abundance of slender, vertical stems, covered in creamy-white flowers in early summer. And finally, *R. pulverulenta* is a wonderfully untypical species rose with richly scented foliage. It reaches about 90 cm (3 ft) and has pink flowers and blood-red hips. The only drawback is that this unusual gem is hard to find.

Above: ***Rosa moyesii,*** from western China, forms a wonderful tangled thicket of a hedge. Prune regularly to keep it dense and to ensure a good supply of winter hips.

Right: **White, single flowers appear in late spring and early summer on the dense, prickly species rose *R. pimpinellifolia*, which spreads by suckers.**

species roses gallery

R. banksiae var. banksiae

H: to 10 m (33 ft).

With its generous clusters of small white scented flowers, this species rambler is the perfect choice for a glorious late spring to early summer display. Grow up a strong tree or wall. Needs a warm, sheltered garden.

R. banksiae 'Lutea'

H: to 10 m (33 ft).

A vigorous, arching rose that produces abundant showers of fully double, clear yellow blooms, carried in dense clusters, from late spring to early summer. It is the hardiest of the Banksian roses, but still requires a sheltered, frost-free position. A graceful, elegant beauty with slender, almost thornless stems.

R. brunonii 'La Mortola'

H: to 7.5 m (25 ft).

A massive, vigorous climbing rose that spreads as wide as it is high, producing masses of excellent white flowers and thousands of thorny prickles. Grown up against garden boundaries, it provides excellent security, as its thicket of thorns will repel all but the most determined intruder. It demands a warm garden, free of hard frosts.

R. glauca

H: to 2.5 m (8 ft).

A beautiful, elegant rose that is more like a willowy young tree than a shrubby species rose. The delicately tinged steel-blue leaves make a harmonious backdrop for the subtle pale pink flowers. Clusters of red hips follow in autumn. It needs a specially selected spot in the border where adjacent tall growth is kept away so that its graceful, wand-like form can be properly appreciated.

R. helenae

H: to 6 m (20 ft).

This is a wonderful climber for growing over hedges or into old trees, scrambling along and anchoring itself into place with its vicious thorns. It is an unusual eye-catcher, bearing rounded clusters of vanilla-white flowers highlighted by dark green leaves.

R. moyesii

H: to 3.7 m (12 ft).

One of the best species roses, this forms a well-shaped upright shrub, studded in the summer months with large, flat, rich red flowers with a rich fringe of golden stamens at the centre. The flowers are followed by a profusion of large, bright red hips. Makes a very good hedge, but also excellent grown as a specimen plant.

R. rugosa

H: to 2.2 m (7 ft).

A tough, vigorous rose that grows to form a very dense, impenetrable hedge. The first burst of flowering occurs in early summer, followed by a succession of flowers through to autumn. The vivid, scented, purple-rose blooms are followed by large, handsome, bright red hips, which are attractive to birds and sometimes appear in combination with later flowers. Never prune or dead-head a rugosa, as this will result in stunted growth and no hips. Rugosas have excellent disease resistance.

R. sericea subsp. omeiensis f. pteracantha

H: to 2.5 m (8 ft).

This shrubby species rose can be grown as a hedge or as a specimen plant in the border. The small white flowers and well-defined, glossy green leaves are pretty enough, but this rose's main attraction is its dramatic, large, translucent, triangular red thorns, which stud the slender stems. To highlight this curious feature, it is best to position the rose where the light will shine through the thorns.

R. wichurana

H: to 2 m (6½ ft).

This climber can be grown over hedges and into trees, or used to provide very impressive ground cover, providing a wide, thick mound of flowers and leaves. It flowers in late summer, producing loose clusters of cupped, single white flowers with prominent golden-yellow stamens and a distinct whiff of clover. In autumn, long, ovoid, tomato-red hips dangle in groups among the leaves.

Top left: **R. banksiae 'Lutea'**

Top right: **R. glauca**

Above left: **R. moyesii**

Above centre: **R. rugosa 'Alba'**

Far right: **R. sericea subsp. omeiensis f. pteracantha**

Right: **R. helenae**

Opposite page: **R. rugosa**

Old garden roses are shrub roses with a graceful, lax habit. They have a strong constitution, and are surprisingly easy to grow. Their evocative names recall a past era of grandeur and graciousness, as do their satiny, blowsy flowers in resplendent tones of crimson, scarlet, purple and pink.

old garden roses

The Old garden roses are made up of several different groups, which include some of the most beautiful and exquisite of all roses. They can be divided into two groups, those that repeat flower and those that do not. Five groups, the Gallicas, Albas, Centifolias, Mosses and some Damasks, do not repeat flower, whilst some Damasks, the Chinas, Portlands, Bourbons, Hybrid Perpetuals and Teas do. In addition to their beautiful, luscious flowers, many of the Old garden roses have powerful, rich scents.

Right: **'Mme Isaac Pereire' is a magnificent Bourbon rose whose huge purplish pink flowers have a delectable scent. This is a vigorous rose, growing to about 2.2 m (7 ft) tall, and the more support you give it the better.**

Old garden roses have powerful, rich scents.

Above: **The beautiful, early 19th-century Alba 'Königin von Dänemark' ('Queen of Denmark') carries double, fragrant flowers.**

Far right: *Rosa* **'Louise Odier' is a repeat-flowering Old rose par excellence, blooming from early summer to late autumn. Support is required to stop the heavy flowers bending the stems right over.**

The Albas

If you need a reliable, disease-free, minimum-attention Old rose for a shady spot, choose one of the Albas. They grow to about 1.8 m (6 ft) high, make a decent hedge, and used to be known as Tree roses because they stand so upright. These vigorous roses flower once in mid-summer. The only care they need is some top pruning in early spring to encourage more growth from the base.

Albas are usually white roses, although some do come in shades of palest pink. One of the very best pink Albas is 'Königin von Dänemark' ('Queen of Denmark'). It is a tall, open, elegant bush with pale pink flowers and a yellow button centre, set against dark grey-green foliage. 'Madame Legras de St. Germain'

is equally outstanding. A fabulous white, tinged with lemon yellow, it gets rave reviews from all the rose experts. It has few thorns and a gorgeous scent.

'Celestial' (or 'Céleste') is rather different because it is at its best when the buds are just unscrolling and opening. Its double flowers, in softest pink, are crammed with about 25 petals, and are beautifully set off by the grey-green leaves. 'Félicité Parmentier' also puts on a fabulous display of buds that open to reveal powder-pink double flowers set against pale green leaves. And 'Great Maiden's Blush' is a superb plant, one of the best shrub roses, with blowsy, satiny flowers in pale pink that fade to creamy-white at the edges of the petals, and a powerful, sweet scent. The dull green foliage is virtually disease resistant.

The best of the smaller Bourbons include 'Souvenir de la Malmaison', 90 cm (3 ft) high, which has gorgeous, delicate, peachy-pink flowers. 'Boule de Neige' is a perfect white, with clusters of round, ball-shaped flowers. It makes the ideal partner for 'Commandant Beaurepaire', also 1.5 m (5 ft) high, which has boldly striped flowers. Good fun if you like pink, purple and scarlet set against pale green leaves. 'Variegata di Bologna' grows higher, to 2.2 m (7 ft), and is also striped, in palest pink and crimson. It is not quite as arresting, but both roses are guaranteed to liven things up in the border. 'Reine Victoria' is also highly popular – it grows to 1.5 m (5 ft) high and is graceful and arching with deep rose-pink flowers and a delicious, heady scent.

Bourbon roses

The Bourbons are a marvellous varied group of repeat-flowering shrub roses with long summer flowering and strong scent. Their opulent, blowsy double flowers have the classic Old rose look. The first Bourbon was found on the island of Réunion in 1817, a cross between the repeat-flowering 'Old Blush' China and a Damask.

If you rate scent highly, 'Mme Isaac Pereire' is the perfect choice. The large flowers are crimson-pink tinged with purple, and the final burst of flowers in the autumn is a spectacular sight. The 2.2 m (7 ft) stems mean that this rose can be grown as a climber. 'Louise Odier' is slightly shorter, with camellia-like flowers in a gentle pink, the petals arranged in circles, one within the other.

The Centifolias

Centifolias produce large flowers on lax, arching stems in mid-summer. Despite their obvious charms, they can be frustrating roses to grow. The scent is amazing and the mainly pink flowers are luscious, but the growth can be disappointing. The long, lax stems need support, especially when weighed down by the heavy flowers. The problem can be pre-empted by pruning half the length in early spring.

'Fantin-Latour' is one of the best Centifolias. Named after the 19th-century French painter, this is a genuine beauty with profuse petals, a strong, sweet scent and lavish pale pink blooms, making a nicely shaped, rounded bush that can reach 1.5 m (5 ft) high. It is justifiably extremely popular. 'Tour de Malakoff' is taller, at 2.2 m (7 ft), and is a surprisingly rarely grown star. The flowers are a wonderful rich magenta when they open, fading to a cool violet. *R.* × *centifolia* gets quite a mixed press. It is loved by some, while others dismiss it as the 'old cabbage rose'. It grows 1.5 m (5 ft) high, is covered by numerous rich pink flowers, and has a lovely rich scent.

The last three Centifolias are quite small. 'Robert le Diable', 90 cm (3 ft) high, has lilac-purple flowers patterned with grey and scarlet. It is more subtle than it sounds. The one hiccup is that it hates wet summers. 'Petite de Hollande' and 'De Meaux' grow 1.2 m (4 ft) and 90 cm (3 ft) respectively and are ideal for small beds. Both are pink, and there is little to choose between them.

China roses

Above: **The soft pink, scented and vigorous *R.* × *centifolia* gets a mixed press. Its followers call it 'the rose of a hundred leaves', while the anti-brigade call it 'old cabbage rose'.**

China roses have had perhaps more influence than any other rose group on the way modern roses look and flower. In the late 18th century, they were brought from the Far East to Europe, where rose breeders crossed them with European roses to produce the direct ancestors of the modern rose – plants that combined repeat flowering, good scent and an exquisite, high-pointed shape.

Producing small, delicate flowers, Chinas repeat flower from summer to early autumn. 'Old Blush' is one of the most beautiful Chinas. It has everything: dainty, pink flowers, a faint but delicious scent, a long flowering season in mild conditions, and it can grow to 2.2 m (7 ft), given fertile soil and a sheltered spot. *Rosa* × *odorata* 'Mutabilis' is just as good. Each flower lasts only three days, opening coppery-yellow, turning orange-pink, and ending up red, but every day more and more appear. It reaches 2.5 m (8 ft) and is slightly tender, needing a warm garden.

If you can find the 'Five-coloured China Rose' snap it up. It is not the most vigorous plant, but produces white, pink and red flowers at the same time. And the final China is the lovely 'Hermosa', which is thoroughly hardy, grows to 90 cm (3 ft) high, and has a mass of pink petals: an extremely good little rose.

The Damasks

Damasks are graceful beauties with a delicious strong scent. The generally pink flowers, borne in fine sprays, have a big scent, and appear once in mid-summer, but success requires humus-rich, fertile soil. Growth is open and arching, to about 1.5 m (5 ft) high.

The Damasks with star quality begin with 'Marie Louise'. Its trademark is big, deep pink flowers, so plump and weighty that they bend the stems right down. 'Ispahan' cannot compete in bloom size, but it has a long flowering period, the longest in this group, about six weeks, and produces plenty of large clear pink blooms with a rich, heady scent. 'Madame Hardy' has a double flower that is pure white with a green eye, and is one of the best Old rose whites you will ever see, though since *R. × centifolia* is one of its parents, it is not a true Damask.

'Celsiana' is a typical Damask, with sprays of pink flowers with crinkled petals, and 'La Ville de Bruxelles' has even larger flowers, weighing down the graceful branches, which have to be lifted up to see them clearly. The clear pink 'Quatre Saisons' (with the ridiculously long official name of *R. × damascena* var. *semperflorens*) is not quite in this league, but it flowers all the way through from early summer to mid-autumn.

Above: **The large blush-pink blooms of *R.* 'Ispahan' mingle with white *Lychnis coronaria*. If you like Damasks and need a long flower show, this is the one to chose. 'Ispahan' also makes good cut flowers.**

The Gallicas

Gallicas have richly coloured flowers on a dense, upright shrubby bush. They are also distinguished in having the longest history of any Old garden rose. Their stems are more bristly than thorny, and the wonderfully elegant, moderately scented blooms are in the pink to rich purple range. The flowers appear once a summer. There is a big display, and the abundant and colourful flowers are very impressive. The plants are not too fussy, but they tend to sucker (sending up stems from below ground) and spread. They make very good hedges of about 1.2 m (4 ft) high; and unless stated, that is the height they grow to. Intense breeding meant a handful of Gallicas in the mid-17th century increased to over 1,000 varieties in 200 years. They are irresistibly beautiful border plants.

'Belle de Crécy' is top of the list with rich lilac-pink flowers that gradually soften to pale violet, with a button eye in the centre, a gorgeous scent, and lax growth. Second comes the 1.5 m (5 ft) high 'Charles de Mills', which has precisely rounded crimson flowers but only a moderate scent. 'Complicata' grows taller than the rest, reaching 2.2 m (7 ft), and its flowers are wonderfully different, being rich pink outside, with a blush interior, and yellow stamens in the centre.

The red *R. gallica* var. *officinalis*, the medieval Apothecary's rose, and probably even the red Rose of Lancaster, is a much more traditional Gallica. Quiet at the beginning of the summer, it soon bursts into flower, with the crimson blooms standing out vividly against the dark green leaves. Equally good are the striking, two-toned 'Président de Sèze', whose flowers are lilac at the edge and crimson within, the purple 'Tuscany' and the brash bright pink 'Versicolor', which is marked and striped in red. 'Cardinal de Richelieu' is one of the most richly coloured Gallicas. Its fat buds open pink, but eventually turn a deep wine-purple. It grows 1.5 m (5 ft) high.

If you have room for more Gallicas, 'Assemblage des Beautés' is another excellent choice. Its vivid crimson flowers gradually turn to a rich deep purple. Another beauty is the gorgeous soft pink 'Duchesse de Montebello', which reaches 1.5 m (5 ft) in height. The 90 cm (3 ft) high 'Gloire de France', with large, rounded mauve flowers, lilac at the rim, is another stunner. All are wonderful plants and well worth a spot in the garden.

Above: **The pale blush-pink blooms of** *R. gallica* **'Versicolor' are striped and splashed reddish pink, like a raspberry-ripple ice cream. The rose is even showier grown as a standard.**

Hybrid Perpetuals

Hybrid Perpetuals repeat flower throughout the summer and autumn. They are a concoction of various mixes that were hugely popular during the second half of the 19th century. Few are still grown, but there are one or two crackers remaining. They also generally have good scent. All need humus-rich, fertile soil. For the best displays, train them horizontally or bend them over, tying in the shoots, with flowers appearing right along the length.

The 1.5 m (5 ft) high 'Georg Arends' is a stunner in rose-pink with a fabulous scent. The slightly shorter 'Baron Girod de l'Ain' is a strong, upright plant with dark crimson flowers with a white ring round them and leathery leaves and 'Baronne Prévost' has bright pink double blooms. 'Reine des Violettes' is a real charmer, with velvety purple flowers that gradually soften to lilac. Both of these are about 1.5 m (5 ft) high. For those with poor soil, 'Mrs John Laing' combines vigorous 1.2 m (4 ft) growth with silvery-pink double flowers and strong fragrance.

Moss roses

Moss roses are actually Centifolias but they have a sticky moss-like covering on their stems and calyxes, the result of a sport or mutation. *R. × centifolia* 'Muscosa' was the original Moss rose. It was such a hit at the start of the 18th century that hundreds of varieties were introduced before they fell from fashion. There are now only about 50 Moss roses, but among these are some marvellous plants. They certainly deserve a come-back, being sturdier than the Centifolias, often with strong colours.

'Comtesse de Murinais', 1.5 m (5 ft) high, is a good strong shrub with pink flowers that fade to white and a powerful scent. 'William Lobb' is one of the tallest, nearly 2.5 m (8 ft) high, with a gorgeous mix of hues – the rich purple flowers fade to pinkish-mauve with hints of magenta. This vigorous rose should be kept to the back of the border or tied to an arch. 'René d'Anjou' is smaller at 1.5 m (5 ft), with a heavenly perfume and sugar-pink flowers. It looks terrific beside the dark pink 'Maréchal Davoust'. 'Capitaine John Ingram' also changes colour, from deep red to purple. Also recommended is 'Henri Martin', a lovely crimson.

Right: **If one Portland outshines the rest it is 'Mme Knorr', previously known as 'Comte de Chambord'. It combines upright growth, good fragrance and plenty of flowers all summer.**

Portland roses

Portlands are ideal for smaller gardens and repeatedly provide an excellent show of blossoms during the summer and autumn. This tiny group of plants dates from the end of the 18th century. They have low, compact growth with good repeat flowering, and often good scent. 'Madame Knorr' is the most popular, a lovely scented rose with a rich, velvety pink hue. A fine alternative is the satiny, petal-crammed pink 'Marchesa Boccella'. The deep purple 'Indigo' is just as good. All grow to approximately 1.2 m (4 ft) in height.

The Teas

Tea roses are tender beauties that need protecting from the elements. Unless you have a warm sheltered garden, most are hard to grow, as frost checks their growth. But if you are lucky enough to have the right conditions to grow Tea roses, quite a few are stunners. 'Lady Hillingdon' is the most popular. It has gorgeous, slender, waxy buds and perfectly formed, soft apricot-yellow, richly scented flowers, combined with glossy green leaves. It grows to about 90 cm (3 ft) high.

old garden roses gallery

R. 'Belle de Crécy' (Gallica)

Introduced in 1829. H: 1.2 m (4 ft), S: 90 cm (3 ft).

The mid-summer flowers open as velvety lilac-pink but gradually soften to violet. The stems need supporting. It emits a wonderfully intense, spicy fragrance.

R. 'Céleste' (Alba)

Date of introduction unknown. H: to 1.5 m (5 ft), S: 1.2 m (4 ft).

A vigorous, bushy Alba producing abundant double flowers with a sweet fragrance in a delicate pale pink hue in mid-summer. Good for hedging and mixed borders, and valuable for its tolerance of light shade.

R. 'Commandant Beaurepaire' (Bourbon)

Introduced in 1879. H: 1.5 m (5 ft), S: 1.2 m (4 ft).

This bushy, spreading Bourbon rose carries an abundance of wavy-edged pale green leaves which provide an understated backdrop for the large, fragrant, pale pink flowers, which are streaked with red, purple and white.

R. gallica var. officinalis (Gallica)

Grown since the 13th century. H: 80 cm (32 in), S: 90 cm (3 ft).

The Apothecary's rose produces semi-double flowers in a rich, velvety pinkish-red, which emit a fresh, delicious scent. This ancient rose, with a neat, rounded habit, is perfect for the border and has the additional bonus of red hips in autumn.

R. 'Henri Martin' (Moss)

Introduced in 1863. H: to 1.8 m (6 ft), S: 1.2 m (4 ft).

The large double flowers, in rich crimson, bow down the arching stems of this upright rose. This is a very tolerant rose capable of enduring cold conditions as well as hot, dry summers.

R. 'Indigo' (Portland)

Introduced around 1830. H: to 1.2 m (4 ft), S: 90 cm (3 ft).

Deep purple, sweetly scented flowers are produced by a small, vigorous bush. Mid-summer flowers are followed by further generous bursts into autumn.

R. 'Ispahan' (Damask)

Introduced by 1832. H: 1.5 m (5 ft), S: 1.2 m (4 ft).

An opulent beauty with large blooms crammed with satiny petals, this Damask rose repeat flowers throughout summer and autumn and also has a heady scent.

R. 'Madame Hardy' (Damask)

Introduced in 1832. H: to 1.5 m (5 ft), S: 1.2 m (4 ft).

This exquisite rose flowers in mid-summer, producing white flowers with a green eye and a rich scent.

R. 'Mme Isaac Pereire' (Bourbon)

Introduced in 1881. H: to 2.2 m (7 ft), S: 2 m (6½ ft).

A vigorous, arching rose that repeatedly produces large double flowers from summer to autumn. The blooms are deep purplish-pink, crammed with petals, and sweetly scented. Ideal grown against a trellis.

R. × odorata 'Mutabilis' (China)

Grown in Italy by 1894, exact date of introduction unknown. H: to 2.5 m (8 ft), S: 1.8 m (6 ft).

Plant this where you can appreciate the gorgeous colours, which change from copper-yellow to orange-pink and red. It needs a warm, sheltered spot.

R. 'Président de Sèze' (Gallica)

Grown since the 13th century. H: 80 cm (32 in), S: 90 cm (3 ft).

This vigorous Gallica produces a vivid summer display. The fragrant double flowers are lilac-pink edged with magenta.

R. 'Robert le Diable' (Centifolia)

Dates probably from about 1831. H: to 90 cm (3 ft), S: 90 cm (3 ft).

The scented flowers, in a wonderful range of hues from lilac to grey with scarlet markings, are at their best on warm, dry days.

R. 'William Lobb' (Moss)

Introduced in 1855. H: 1.8 m (6 ft), S: 1.8 m (6 ft).

The size of this rose dictates a position at the back of the border where its crimson-fading-to-violet tones and dark foliage are ideal for purple summer schemes.

Top left: *R.* 'Belle de Crécy'

Top centre: *R.* 'Président de Sèze'

Top right: *R.* 'William Lobb'

Above left: *R.* 'Ispahan'

Above centre: *R.* 'Henri Martin'

Above right: *R.* 'Céleste'

Far left: *R. gallica* var. *officinalis*

Left: *R.* × *odorata* 'Mutabilis'

Opposite page: *R.* 'Mme Isaac Pereire'

Modern shrub roses are graceful and elegant, as well as being larger and more prolific than Modern bush roses. The roses grouped together in this category are extremely diverse, ranging from strong, tough shrubs such as the Rugosas to the beautiful English roses and the graceful Hybrid Musks.

modern shrub roses

Modern shrub roses are a very diverse group and their generous palette of colours means that they produce marvellous splashes of colour in the garden. They are usually larger and more prolific than the Modern bush roses and often have thorny stems. Their loose form means that they are ideally suited to informal mixed border plantings and many of the bigger Modern shrub roses make excellent specimen plants.

They are available in all shapes and sizes, ranging from quite amazingly beautiful specimens to strong, tough shrubs that make very good hedges like the Rugosas. Many date back to the end of the 19th century, whilst others are brand new. There are plenty of winners. The flowers, usually scented, can be single, semi-double or double, and are carried in clusters. Most repeat flower. They will provide an elegant backdrop to any garden and produce colourful and beautiful blooms throughout the summer months.

It is hard to select the best because they are all so good.

English roses

English roses are the most important roses of the late 20th century. Most are bred by David Austin (of David Austin Roses, Shropshire, England), whose aim is to combine the graceful looks and rich scent of the Old garden rose with the wide modern colour range and repeat-flowering ability – everything you need, in fact. It is hard to select the best because they are all so good.

'Gertrude Jekyll' is first rate. It is actually quite deceptive because the relatively small buds open out into impressive-sized pink flowers, with an exquisite fruity scent. 'L. D. Braithwaite' has large, petal-crammed blooms in a very good vivid crimson-red that holds its colour without fading. With its strong, punchy colouring, this is ideal trained as a standard, making an incredibly showy sight throughout the summer months. 'L. D. Braithwaite' also combines very well with the cool white 'Glamis Castle', and both keep flowering through the season. Even better, both are ideal for small gardens, each growing to about 90 cm (3 ft) high.

If you want large flowers, choose 'Lilian Austin', which is fractionally taller that the last two roses mentioned and has broad salmon-pink flowers. Alternatively, the blooms of 'Brother Cadfael' are round and plump, making excellent cut flowers. 'Graham Thomas' has buttery yellow flowers and is one of the best of the yellows. It is a vigorous rose, and can be kept to a decent-sized 1.2 m (4 ft), or trained as a 2.5 m (8 ft) high climber. 'Heritage' has beautiful, almost peony-like, flowers in a terrific soft pink shade, as well as a delicate fresh scent.

Far left: **'L. D. Braithwaite'**, **introduced in 1988, is one of the best red English roses. It holds its colour well, has a decent scent, and flowers again and again.**

Left: **'Graham Thomas' is named after the great British rose expert. Famed for its pure, rich yellow, it looks particularly good with sprays of blue delphiniums.**

Other shrub roses

In addition to the English roses discussed above, Modern shrub roses also include a large number of plants introduced in the last 50 years, many the result of crossing Large-flowered bush roses with Cluster-flowered bush roses. These roses are available in a spectrum of bright colours and are repeat flowerers. Some have climbing forms. They are attractive, reliable and robust. Other shrub roses date back to the turn of the century and beyond, and include the Rugosa roses, with their attractive luxuriant foliage, and the Hybrid Musks. There is no shortage of choice in this category – the big problem is deciding which roses to select.

There are plenty of excellent pinks. 'Marguerite Hilling' is a high-impact rose that produces an abundant display of gorgeous rich pink flowers and forms a 2.2 m (7 ft) high rounded shape. 'Fritz Nobis' is slightly shorter and is at its peak in mid-summer. It has a spicy scent and orange-red hips in the autumn.

'Frühlingsmorgen', which grows to 1.8 m (6 ft), produces an exquisite flat flower with gorgeous yellow petals tinged pale peachy-pink towards the edges. The big flower burst is in early summer, followed by sporadic blooms in early autumn.

'Sarah van Fleet' (often listed as a Rugosa) keeps flowering all summer, emitting a gentle but delicious scent. The cupped flowers have sugar-pink petals and a golden centre. It puts on a packed, dense show of blooms and provides a perfect background for smaller plants, but at 2.5 m (8 ft) high does need plenty of space. 'Lady Curzon' is another tall pink. It grows madly, sending stems in all directions, into trees and over shrubs, and has beautiful, scented flowers. If you need something smaller, 'Sadler's Wells' repeat flowers, and has deep rich pink flowers scattered against glossy green foliage. It grows 1.2 m (4 ft) high.

The stronger crimsons begin with 'Scarlet Fire'. This really lives up to its name, producing a mass of 3 m (10 ft) high growth, studded with wide, velvety flowers and creating a dense mass in

Below left: **'Cerise Bouquet' grows to 2.5 m (8 ft) or even higher, and with its arching stems might need tying in. You know when it is flowering in early summer by its gorgeous raspberry scent.**

Below centre: **The early summer rose 'Nevada', with its profusion of creamy white blooms, perfectly complements the unfurling golden-yellow clusters of the laburnum, and helps to soften the hard lines in this small courtyard garden.**

mid-summer. 'Cerise Bouquet' is another monster, reaching 2.5 m (8 ft) high, and producing bright, punchy flowers that are a cluster of satiny petals in mid-summer. The flowers have a wonderful fruity scent. For smaller borders, combine 'Henry Kelsey', with its fabulous red flowers, glossy foliage and subtle scent, with the crimson 'Mrs Anthony Waterer', which has a wider spread and a richer scent. Both will grow to about 1.2 m (4 ft) high.

To tone down these hothouse colours, mix in some whites and yellows. 'Nevada' is a sensational white for early summer, its 2.5 m (8 ft) high stems thickly covered in large, creamy-white flowers. 'Dupontii' is an early 19th-century beauty that deserves to be much more popular. It grows as tall as 'Nevada' and has beautifully formed pure white flowers in summer, combined with a rich, fruity scent. 'Jacqueline du Pré' will flower reliably from late spring to late autumn. The colour is between ivory and blush, and it has a sweet scent. At 1.5 m (5 ft) high, it is slightly smaller than many shrubs, and makes an outstanding combination with

'Gertrude Jekyll'. 'Sir Frederick Ashton' is another marvellous, smaller white, reaching 1.2 m (4 ft), and even smaller but no less excellent is 'Little White Pet', which reaches about 60 cm (2 ft) and can also be grown as a standard – it will form a neat, compact ball that is studded with white flowers all summer long. Plant four standards around a circular herb garden, with another in the centre, for an elegant and formal effect. 'Little White Pet' has a profusion of pretty pompom flowers, which appear regularly during its long flowering season, and there is no excuse for not finding it a space in your garden.

The same goes for the yellow 'Golden Wings'. At 1.5 m (5 ft) high, it flowers for most of the summer, producing lemon-yellow single flowers with a tangy scent. 'Frühlingsgold' also gets top marks on most counts; it flowers in early summer, sometimes followed by a token autumn show. The 1.8 m (6 ft) stems are packed with large primrose-yellow flowers, and the strong scent is unbelievable. It gets summer off to an incredible start.

Below right: **A shrub rose of spreading habit, 'Raubritter' makes an excellent ground-cover rose. Here the pink summer flowers are teamed with delphiniums.**

Ground-cover roses

These roses will scramble far and wide, but they do not actually hug the ground like ivy or other ground-covering perennials, so cannot suppress weeds. However, they do form spreading, dense shrubs and look wonderful in a border or tumbling gracefully down a wall. Ground-cover roses are ideal for slopes and grassy banks. Many are repeat flowerers, and provide a carpet of colour throughout the summer months.

The pink 'Max Graf' is close to perfect. It will spread and sprawl as far as 2.5 m (8 ft), rooting as it grows, rarely reaching above 90 cm (3 ft) high and making a highly effective cover. If you want something even more vigorous, choose 'Pleine de Grâce', which will spread as far as 3.7 m (12 ft), and is absolutely covered with white flowers in mid-summer. It is well scented and has attractive hips in autumn. On a smaller scale, there is the delicate lavender 'Magic Carpet', which covers about 1.2 m (4 ft), and the marvellous 'Nozomi', which is about the same size. 'Raubritter', at 1.8 m (6 ft) across, is a very special ground-cover rose. The flowers are a tight ball of overlapping petals, opening to reveal an exquisitely formed, rich pink bloom.

Hybrid Musks

Do not be misled by the name – these roses are not relatives of the Musk rose. With their massed, large sprays of flowers, which appear through the summer, they look more similar to Cluster-flowered bush roses. The Hybrid Musks were developed between 1900 and 1930, and were largely the creation of a German rose breeder, Peter Lambert, and the Revd. Joseph Pemberton, although their original roses have now largely been been replaced by others. The Hybrid Musks have one hefty flowering spell in early summer, followed by a scattering of flowers through the season, and many also have good scent. Few gardeners have heard of the group name, but one or two Hybrid Musks really are absolute stunners, and would make an excellent addition to any garden. Hybrid Musks generally reach a height of around 1.8–2.2 m (6–7 ft), and need plenty of humus-rich compost to flourish.

'Buff Beauty' is perhaps the most well-known Hybrid Musk. It has apricot-yellow flowers, freely appearing from mid-summer into autumn, set against highly attractive dark green foliage with reddish shoots. At 1.8 m (6 ft) high, it makes a perfect scented hedge. The same can be said for 'Cornelia', which is only marginally smaller, and produces enormous sprays of deep apricot flowers that fade to a gentle sugar-pink. The autumn colour is even better. The sweetly scented flowers are excellent for cutting.

'Penelope' is an interesting choice for both a hedge and a specimen planting. It has rich orange buds that open to reveal pink-flushed flowers that fade to white, followed by hips that turn from green to pink. A terrific range of hues from one plant, which will make a hedge about 1.2 m (6 ft) high. 'Vanity' is a large rose that can also be grown as a climber, with strong pink flowers opening from lipstick-pink buds. The scent is similar to that of a sweet pea. 'Wilhelm', 2.2 m (7 ft) high, is a vivid crimson hue. It has hardly any scent, but its tomato-red hips, which persist throughout the winter, make up for this. If you have a smaller garden, try 'Ballerina', 1.2 m (4 ft) high, another high-impact rose covered in sprays of plentiful pink flowers from mid-summer to autumn. It is also wonderful grown as a standard. Alternatively, if you want a stronger colour, try 'Marjorie Fair', which is an intense carmine with a white eye.

Left: **A gentle approach to a border, with gravel giving way to** Alchemilla mollis **self-seeding in every possible space, then the profuse clusters of apricot-yellow flowers and dark, glossy foliage of 'Buff Beauty'.**

Below: **You would never guess that the 'Ballerina' rose with its mop-head clusters**

belongs to the same group as 'Buff Beauty', but a Hybrid Musk it is, and a good one. 'Ballerina' flowers well all summer, and also makes a first-rate standard.

Right: **Introduced by the French in 1901, the inimitable crimson-purple 'Roseraie de l'Haÿ' is a vigorous Rugosa.**

The Rugosas

The Rugosas are dense, hardy, tallish plants, perfect for any garden, either in a hedge (*see page 75*), growing in a great burst out of the lawn, or arching over the back of a bed. They have luxuriant foliage and flower off and on throughout the summer, producing blooms that last a couple of days, mainly with good scent, and followed by generous clusters of bright autumn hips. Rugosas are good-natured, easy-going roses with a robust constitution and excellent disease resistance – they do not need much pruning and do not even demand first-rate soil. Give them some space and away they go – their only drawback is their spiky, savage thorns.

'Roseraie de l'Haÿ' is probably the most famous Rugosa. It forms a marvellous, big, gap-filling shrub, pumping out flat, double, crimson-purple flowers, 10 cm (4 in) across, with a velvety texture. This shrub will grow to 1.5 m (5 ft) and makes a fine hedge, especially planted beside the clear pink 'Sarah van Fleet' or the pure white 'Blanche Double de Coubert'. These three all flower over the summer, emitting gorgeous, rich scents. A good Rugosa for a smaller garden is the new 'Mrs Doreen Pike', an exceptionally pretty pink rose that reaches just 90 cm (3 ft) high.

modern shrub roses
gallery

R. 'Blanche Double de Coubert'

Introduced in 1892.

H: 1.5 m (5 ft), S: 1.2 m (4 ft).

This Rugosa rose has a dense, spreading habit and the rugged constitution of its wild parent. It produces abundant semi-double pure white blooms, with delicate petals and golden stamens, throughout the summer, as well as large, rounded red hips in autumn.

R. 'Buff Beauty'

Introduced in 1939.

H: 1.8 m (6 ft), S: 1.8 m (6 ft).

A profusion of beige-apricot tinted flowers appear from mid-summer. A second attractive feature is the thick dark green leaves. This Hybrid musk is dense enough to make an impenetrable hedge, but also an excellent addition to a mixed border.

R. 'Frühlingsgold'

Introduced in 1937.

H: to 2.5 m (8 ft), S: 2 m (6½ ft).

A tough, arching rose that will thrive in most soils. A must for early summer, producing a dramatic display of flowers, often followed by more blooms in autumn. The fully double, scented flowers are primrose-yellow with golden stamens, the petals fading to ivory-white in hot and sunny conditions.

R. 'Gertrude Jekyll'

Introduced in 1986.

H: 1.5 m (5 ft), S: 90 cm (3 ft).

An English rose with deceptively small buds that open to reveal impressively sized clear deep pink flowers with a fruity scent, well set off by the thick, dark green foliage. The crammed mass of petals creates a wonderfully opulent, old-fashioned effect.

R. 'Golden Wings'

Introduced in 1956.

H: 1.2 m (4 ft), S: 1.2 m (4 ft).

This elegant arching shrub carries an abundance of sweetly scented, single, saucer-shaped flowers in a rich yellow, the warm colour contrasting well with the bronze stamens. A hardy plant that is excellent for hedging and will flourish on less fertile soils or sites in light shade.

R. 'Graham Thomas'

Introduced in 1983.

H: 1.2 m (4 ft), S: 1.2 m (4 ft).

Named after the great British rose authority, Graham Stuart Thomas, this English rose produces first-rate peony-like blooms in a rich warm yellow, crammed with petals. The large flowers are extremely attractive and sweetly fragrant, so perfect for cutting. Excellent trained as a standard.

R. 'Jacqueline du Pré'

Introduced in 1989.

H: 1.5 m (5 ft), S: 1.5 m (5 ft).

A hugely valuable shrub that flowers from late spring to late autumn. It produces an abundance of dainty blush-white semi-double flowers with prettily scalloped petals, red-gold stamens and a light scent. This versatile rose is good for borders, hedges or grown against a wall. Prefers moist soil.

R. 'L. D. Braithwaite'

Introduced in 1988.

H: 90 cm (3 ft), S: 90 cm (3 ft).

A lavish English rose that bears fragrant flowers right through summer, in an eye-catching crimson that does not fade. Dull dark greyish-green leaves provide an understated backdrop.

R. 'Nevada'

Introduced in 1927.

H: 2.5 m (8 ft), S: 2.5 m (8 ft).

A hugely impressive sight, a great blanket of creamy, pink-flushed flowers in early summer. Second flushes appear in warm weather. Needs plenty of space, so do not try to pack it into a small area.

R. 'Roseraie de l'Haÿ'

Introduced in 1901.

H: 1.5 m (5 ft), S: 1.5 m (5 ft).

A prolific flowering Rugosa, in dark wine-red, that will tolerate quite poor soil and coastal conditions. Strongly scented. Makes a highly impressive flowering hedge.

Top left: *R.* **'Jacqueline du Pré'**

Top centre: *R.* **'Roseraie de l'Haÿ'**

Top right: *R.* **'Nevada'**

Above left: *R.* **'Graham Thomas'**

Above centre: *R.* **'Gertrude Jekyll'**

Above right: *R.* **'Blanche Double de Coubert'**

Left: *R.* **'Buff Beauty'**

Right: *R.* **'Golden Wings'**

Opposite page: *R.* **'Frühlingsgold'**

Modern bush roses can be divided into two main groups: the Large-flowered bush roses, also known as Hybrid Teas, and the Cluster-flowered bush roses, also known as Floribundas. Since the turn of the century, Large-flowered roses have gradually come to dominate the modern rose market.

large-flowered roses

Large-flowered bush roses are perhaps better known as Hybrid Teas. They are a cross between Western and Eastern roses. Tea Roses were first brought to Europe from China towards the end of the 18th century. No-one knows exactly where the Tea name originated. Some rose experts believe that it comes from the Chinese nursery where the roses were obtained, which may have been named something like 'Fa Tee'. Other experts suggest that Tea roses were originally given this name due to the fact that their scent is faintly reminiscent of fresh tea. And some rose experts claim that Tea roses owe their name to the fact that they were brought to Europe by tea merchants, alongside their main cargo. Either way, the Tea roses offered fine, high-pointed flower buds combined with repeat flowering and a gentle but pleasing scent. When they were crossed with Hybrid Perpetuals, the invaluable qualities of robustness, good disease resistance and vigour were added to the Tea's flowering and scent. The result of this pairing, the Hybrid Tea, possessed almost every virtue.

The first Hybrid Tea rose is believed to be 'La France', which was introduced in France in 1867. Initially, there was little interest, but since the turn of the century Hybrid Teas have gradually come to dominate the rose market. Thousands have been introduced, thousands rejected and thousands have vanished, with constant improvements taking place. The colour range is constantly being increased – yellow was first introduced, then vermilion, providing an exciting palette of new, brighter hues. The Hybrid Teas' only possible defect is their vulnerability to rain damage. And some

Below: **Clumps of Large-flowered roses are punctuated by the towering spires of delphiniums. A setting such as this calls for plants that can compete, so choose robust, vigorous roses that offer long flowering and good scent.**

varieties were so geared towards producing a perfect, prize-winning flower shape that the plant lacked garden presence. Now, however, breeders are putting this right.

A whole bed devoted to Hybrid Teas may seem like a wonderful idea, but be warned – they can be thunderingly monotonous together, and out of season are all bare, stalky twigs and brown earth. To prevent this effect, combine them with grasses, geraniums, alchemilla and delphiniums, or with clumps of herbs and lavenders, so their leggy outlines are softened and they are drawn into the garden scheme. All the Hybrid Teas flower with summer and autumn bursts, producing sporadic blooms in between. The scent is incredibly variable. The majority grow to approximately 90 cm (3 ft) high.

Above: **'Alec's Red' has picked up awards for its good looks and rich scent. If the colour suits, buy it.**

Above right: **The dusky scarlet 'Fragrant Cloud' is one of the best scented Modern roses. It is not, alas, disease resistant.**

Reds

There are some excellent red Hybrid Teas on offer with very little to choose between them. 'Royal William' is a 1987 introduction that has been a huge success. The deep crimson flowers are well-shaped, large and scented and the long stalks make it an excellent cut flower. 'Loving Memory' is equally good, with vivid pink-crimson flowers, and, with its large, dark green leaves, perhaps looks better in the garden.

There are some excellent red Hybrid Teas on offer.

If scent is all-important, choose 'Fragrant Cloud'. It might be prone to black spot but is an absolute star, producing an abundance of orange-red blooms. 'Ena Harkness' is similar, with good scent, rich deep scarlet-crimson flowers, and a wonderful velvety texture to the petals. It provides a fine autumn show, though the flowers tend to hang down. And, if you need one more, 'Alec's Red' has superb scent and large bright poppy-red flowers that are beautifully formed.

Pinks

'Warm Wishes' (or 'Sunset Celebration', as it is called in America) won the 1998 All American Rose Selection Award as well as nine other international awards, including one for fragrance. The large peach-coloured flowers, flushed with apricot, keep appearing all summer long, and are set off perfectly by the dark green foliage. 'Silver Jubilee' is another quality Hybrid Tea. The graceful flowers are perfectly shaped and a strong sugar-pink shade. Since its 1978 introduction, this has been a big seller.

'Savoy Hotel' is another recent hit. Introduced in 1989, it is a vigorous, bushy rose that produces large, fully double flowers in classic pale pink. It produces generous amounts of flowers – enough blooms to pick and to leave for a good garden show. 'Elizabeth Harkness' is an exquisite beauty dating back to the late 1960s. The elegant blooms are a rich creamy-pink, faintly amber-tinted, fading to blush at the edges of the petals. It starts flowering in early summer, and continues right through the season. As it unfolds, 'Lovely Lady' is flushed with creamy-apricot, but it opens to reveal a rose-pink bloom. This beauty has large flowers, a sweet scent, and a vigorous form. It might not win first prize in a show, but in the garden it can hardly be bettered. And finally, 'My Joy' is a top exhibiting rose, with rich pink flowers, perfectly shaped and well displayed on a bold, upright bush.

Orange and salmon

This colour combination offers some amazing effects. 'Whisky Mac' may not be the strongest, most reliable rose, for it is prone to various diseases, but where it thrives it will provide a spectacular show, with an abundance of dazzling two-tone flowers in gold and amber that make it an enormous favourite. 'Just Joey' was voted the World's Favourite Rose in 1994. It is perfectly formed and has an abundance of slightly wavy edged, copper-orange flowers that emit a decent scent and will withstand rain. Both of these roses will bring an injection of colour and excitement to the border.

'Remember Me' may not be quite as spectacular, but it is still worth a place in most gardens. The scent is minimal, but the large orange flowers, with copper and peach tones, appear in clusters, creating a generous and dramatic effect. 'Rosemary Harkness' is a cheery blend of creamy-peach and salmon-orange, and 'New Zealand' is a complete contrast. The salmon-pink colouring is subtle and unobtrusive, and it needs carefully chosen companions that will complement rather than overpower it.

Above: **Voted the World's Favourite Rose in 1994, 'Just Joey' is a prolific flowerer, stands up to the rain and is disease resistant. The fragrant copper-pink flowers fade to creamy-orange.**

Left: **The all-purpose, won't-let-you-down pink rose, 'Lovely Lady'. At 75 x 75 cm (2½ x 2½ ft) it tucks neatly into the front of the border, where you can snip off the large blooms and get a good whiff of its strong scent.**

Yellows

Yellow Hybrid Teas are extremely versatile – they will blend well with other reds and oranges in the border for a no-nonsense 'hot' scheme, contrast gently with blues and mauves and dark red-blacks, and blend into cottage-garden pinks and whites. 'Peace' has long been the all-time favourite. A 1942 French introduction, it set new standards when first launched, with bigger flowers and increased vigour. It grows up to 1.2 m (4 ft) high (even taller if left unpruned) and has glossy foliage teamed with large yellow flowers tinged with pink. All it lacks is a powerful scent. 'Dutch Gold' is a fragranced alternative, with large, scented golden-yellow flowers that will withstand heavy rain without becoming totally bedraggled.

Two much more recent yellows that are well worth growing are 'Freedom' and 'Tequila Sunrise'. 'Freedom' cannot be bettered for bedding – the egg-yolk yellow flowers show up wonderfully against the abundant shiny leaves. 'Tequila Sunrise' may be a little gaudy for some tastes, but for new colour seekers it mixes peachy-apricot yellow with bright scarlet edging. For something far gentler, choose 'Elina' (formerly known as 'Peaudouce') for its soft ivory flowers tinted with lemon-yellow, and a light scent that is sweet but elusive. This is also wonderful grown as a standard, forming a compact ball studded with yellow-white blooms.

Whites

There are not a huge number of top-quality white Hybrid Teas, but 'Polar Star' is up there among the best. Bred in Germany in 1982, it was an immediate winner, with strong, vigorous growth and shapely, high-pointed buds, faintly green, which open to reveal a perfectly formed, creamy-white flower. Alas, unlike 'Evening Star' and 'Pristine', it has no scent. These two roses have pure white flowers that stand out well against the dark green leaves. The scented 'Ice Cream', with its white flowers flushed yellow, goes one step better because it has new foliage in a dull red hue that turns brownish green when mature.

Above: **With its double yellow flowers edged with scarlet set against dark glossy leaves, 'Tequila Sunrise' shows rose breeders exactly what can be achieved.**

Right: **'Peace' is a fine vigorous rose that set new standards in 1942. The double yellow flowers are tinged with pink and have a delicate fragrance.**

large-flowered roses gallery

R. 'Elina'

Introduced in 1985.

H: 1.2 m (4 ft), S: 90 cm (3 ft).

A near-perfect rose, equally good in the garden and on the show bench. It produces exquisite, large flowers, 15 cm (6 in) across, in creamy-primrose-yellow. The colour fades, which is why some rose catalogues list it as a white rose. This beauty is easy to grow and even withstands the rain. Its only drawback is its almost non-existent scent.

R. 'Elizabeth Harkness'

Introduced in 1969.

H: 75 cm (2½ ft) high, S: 75 cm (2½ ft).

This pert, upright bush flowers without any breaks over the summer, producing an abundance of gentle, creamy-pinkish flowers, 13 cm (5 in) wide. A hardy rose tolerant of a wide range of conditions.

R. 'Ena Harkness'

Introduced in 1946.

H: 75 cm (2½ ft), S: 75 cm (2½ ft).

This top-notch scented rose is ideal for hot red borders. The urn-shaped, rich crimson flowers, with their velvety petals, do not fade as they age. Flowers recurrently all summer long and into autumn.

R. 'Peace'

Introduced in 1942.

H: 1.2 m (4 ft), S: 90 cm (3 ft).

Perhaps the most famous rose ever bred and still an excellent and very popular choice. It grows to form a robust and vigorous bush with opulent, luscious flowers 15 cm (6 in) wide. The pale yellow blooms have waved petals tinged with pink at the edges and appear from summer to autumn. An excellent all-rounder, ideal for beds, borders, hedging, cutting and exhibiting.

R. 'Polar Star'

Introduced in 1982.

H: 90 cm (3 ft), S: 75 cm (2½ ft).

One of the best Hybrid Tea whites with well-shaped, pointed, creamy-white flowers freely appearing on strong, sturdy stems. Robust, reliable and easy to grow.

R. 'Remember Me'

Introduced in 1984.

H: 90 cm (3 ft), S: 75 cm (2½ ft).

A vigorous rose with a dense, upright habit and an abundance of small glossy leaves. The flowers are fully double and perfectly shaped, carried above stiff stems. They are a deep coppery-orange shade with a light scent, excellent for cutting.

R. 'Royal William'

Introduced in 1987.

H: 75 cm (2½ ft), S: 60 cm (2 ft).

With large flowers, 13 cm (5 in) across, in a rich deep red hue, this Hybrid Tea takes some beating. The large, shiny, deep green leaves are a perfect foil for the deep crimson blooms. Ideal for cut flowers, especially as it has a gentle but delicious scent.

R. 'Silver Jubilee'

Introduced in 1978.

H: 90 cm (3 ft), S: 60 cm (2 ft).

This hugely popular rose is immaculate in every way, with a perfect, pointed form and silvery-pink petals set against plentiful dark green leaves. Puts on a wonderful show, flowering from summer through to autumn. Just one in any small space will do.

R. 'Tequila Sunrise'

Introduced in 1989.

H: 75 cm (2½ ft), S: 60 cm (2 ft).

Recently, rose breeders have produced Hybrid Teas in increasingly dramatic and unusual hues. This rose has deep orange-yellow flowers, the petals rimmed with a thick border of fiery scarlet. It flowers throughout the summer and into autumn. It is well suited to beds, borders and growing as a standard.

R. 'Whisky Mac'

Introduced in 1967.

H: 75 cm (2½ ft), S: 60 cm (2 ft).

A fussy and particular rose that has quite beautiful flowers in a rich golden amber. Its exquisite colouring makes it well worth seeking out a special position with humus-rich soil and good drainage.

Left: *R.* **'Tequila Sunrise'**

Below left: *R.* **'Elina'**

Below centre: *R.* **'Royal William'**

Below right: *R.* **'Whisky Mac'**

Bottom left: *R.* **'Peace'**

Bottom centre: *R.* **'Silver Jubilee'**

Bottom right: *R.* **'Polar Star'**

Opposite page: *R.* **'Remember Me'**

Cluster-flowered bush roses, or Floribundas, were produced by crossing cluster-flowered Polyantha roses with Hybrid Teas. Borne in trusses, the flowers of these upright roses open one after the other. So as old blooms fade, new ones appear to give a long flowering period of continual blooms.

cluster-flowered roses

Cluster-flowered bush roses is a grand name for the group of roses that are still more commonly known as Floribundas. These were pioneered by the 20th-century Danish hybridist Svend Poulsen. They produce a cluster of blooms on a stem, providing a constant, massed effect of smallish flowers. Compared to the larger Hybrid Teas, they are not quite as show-bench beautiful, or as strongly scented, but for dependable, regular garden colour and a cluster of flowers, they are perfect.

The first Floribundas were the red 'Kirsten Poulsen' and the pink 'Else Poulsen', which were introduced in 1924, the result of crossing a Polyantha and Hybrid Tea. Since then, hundreds of Floribundas have been developed, involving genes from all types of roses. If you have a border that needs a bit of oomph, try a Floribunda. They have good disease resistance and are reliably hardy. On average they reach about 90 cm (3 ft) in height.

If you have got a border that needs a bit of oomph, try a Floribunda.

Above: **It's now almost impossible to find a nursery that sells 'Else Poulsen'. It's a great shame because this 1924 pink rose, one of the first Floribundas, is a quiet, gentle beauty.**

Left: **The best way to give extra height to a bright, punchy 60 cm (2 ft) high rose, like this 'Trumpeter', is to grow it in a raised bed. And as it is so small, you can have fun angling long, pointy phormium leaves over it.**

Bold reds

There are plenty of first-rate red Floribundas to choose from. 'Trumpeter' will provide a blast of intense vermilion at the front of the border and flowers unstintingly throughout summer and autumn. The abundance of blooms means that there are more than enough flowers brightening up the garden as well as for cutting. Grow it as a standard and it will be a wonderfully flamboyant sight in full flower. The slightly larger 'Beautiful Britain' is an eye-catching bright tomato-red colour; disease resistant and healthy, this is a rose you cannot fail with. If you prefer a red with a hint of orange, then 'Melody Maker' is ideal. It forms a neatly shaped bush and from summer through to autumn produces poppy-red flowers with an orange tint. They stand out sharply against the dark, glossy leaves.

For those wanting plenty of cut flowers, 'Europeana' is the answer. It produces an amazing number of flowers, so many that the slender stems bend over beneath the weight. Do look out for mildew, though. Finally, 'The Times Rose' is another excellent Floribunda, with dark red flowers made up of velvety crimson petals. Its shiny, thick foliage builds into a neat bushy shape.

Pinks

'Sexy Rexy' pumps out so many flowers during the summer that it can be difficult to spot the foliage through the mass of blooms. The flowers are a soft candyfloss-pink and are beautifully formed, with a camellia-like shape of curving petals. 'Queen Elizabeth' was developed in America in the 1950s and has been a constant best-seller ever since. At 1.7 m (5½ ft), it is exceptionally vigorous, and provides sugar-pink flowers set among a mass of large, shiny leaves. A massed planting of seven or more could create a wonderful garden divide. 'Pink Parfait' is another, slightly smaller,

American stunner, thickly covered with soft pink flowers and thornless stems – excellent for cutting.

If fragrance is a top priority, try 'City of London', 'English Miss' or 'Chanelle'. The first can reach almost double the size of the typical Floribunda if snipped over rather than given a heavy pruning, and has shell-pink flowers with golden eyes. The second produces large sprays of flowers in a gentle peachy-pink and has excellent disease resistance. The third is a creamy-pink verging on beige. The three together would make an elegant bed.

Below left: **'Pink Parfait' is a handsome combination of open pink flowers set against dark green leaves. It also offers abundant cut flowers all summer.**

Below: **The pale pink, sweet-scented 'English Miss' has a neat, spreading habit, and with its shiny, healthy foliage, it makes a good link between strong, hot colours.**

'Pink Parfait' is a stunner, thickly covered with pink flowers.

Orange, apricot and salmon-pink

'Apricot Nectar' is one of those Floribundas that looks like a Hybrid Tea. The peachy-yellow flowers, grouped in small sprays, are relatively large and have a gentle scent. 'Fragrant Delight' has a bit more presence. The scent is stronger, the colour richer, and the overall effect embellished by masses of glossy, luxuriant foliage. 'Sunset Boulevard' provides a happy medium, with clusters of salmon-pink flowers. And if you want a highly distinctive rose, 'Oranges and Lemons', a golden-yellow rose striped with orange markings is, depending on your taste, either intolerably naff or absolutely stunning. For those who get up close, there is a sweet but gentle scent.

Right: **A graceful white 'Iceberg' has been given plenty of space to perform, whilst contrasting red and yellow roses have been planted in the foreground. 'Iceberg' can keep flowering into early winter.**

Above: **If you are looking to pack an island bed with one rose, try the salmon-pink 'Fragrant Delight' which mixes good scent with leaves that quickly turn shiny, and strong, upright growth.**

Purples and mauves

There are relatively few true purple or mauve roses, but 'Lilac Charm' possesses a gentle scent and and enough colour and charm to qualify for a purple border. 'News' certainly ought to be included. It has stronger purple tones with a mix of beetroot, and yellow stamens, whilst 'Shocking Blue' is not a blue at all but deep mauve. It scores heavily if you are looking for scent.

Whites

One of the most exquisite whites is 'Margaret Merril'. Even those gardeners who do not rate Floribundas want this one. It has immaculate, perfectly sculptured pure white flowers, and excellent, strong scent. It is perfect for a small, spare piece of soil where you want to create an elegant touch. Underplant with blue *Viola cornuta*, which flowers from spring to summer, growing 15 cm (6 in) high and spreading three times as much. Alternatively, more voguishly, choose *Viola tricolor* 'Bowles Black'. This rose is most impressive grown as a standard, providing a nice touch if used as a centrepiece. The big alternative white Floribunda is 'Iceberg', which has enjoyed enormous popularity for the past 40 years. Do not be misled by the pink buds, they open to reveal creamy-white flowers with a very slight, sweet scent. At 1.2 m (4 ft) high, it makes an impressive specimen plant, and is wonderful grown as a standard.

One of the most exquisite whites is 'Margaret Merril'.

Yellows

There are plenty of bright, eye-catching yellow Floribundas that can be planted among cool greens and silver-greys, soft blues, or hot, fiery reds. 'Korresia' is one of the best, with golden-yellow, double, medium-to-large flowers that appear in clusters, with a wonderfully clear colour and rich scent. The American 'Golden Wedding' has flowers that are like those of a Hybrid Tea, high pointed and stylish, in a rich custard-yellow shade, although the delicate scent can be hard to pick up. For softer schemes, 'Great Ormond Street' is another handsome choice. The flowers, as they open, are a bright, strong yellow that gradually fades, softening and turning to rich cream. They are set off by plenty of dark green foliage. If you need something larger, more like a shrub, grow 'Mountbatten', which produces large, tidy blooms in a pale creamy-yellow. It needs little fussing, and is remarkably disease resistant. At 1.2 m (4 ft) high, it can be grown to make an attractive medium-sized hedge.

cluster-flowered roses gallery

R. 'Apricot Nectar'

Introduced in 1965.

H: 90 cm (3 ft), S: 75 cm (2½ ft).

A popular Floribunda that produces open flowers in a pale salmon-pink that tones harmoniously with most other colours. This understated, gentle beauty is ideal for romantic 'cottage garden' type planting schemes. It give its best in fertile, moisture-retentive soil.

R. 'Golden Wedding'

Introduced in 1992.

H: 75 cm (2½ ft), S: 60 cm (2 ft).

A bushy rose with attractive glossy foliage and broad, round, shapely flowers in a delicious rich yellow. It looks good in both formal, stylized layouts and with taller, wispy shapes behind, and is happy in a pot.

R. 'Korresia'

Introduced in 1974.

H: 75 cm (2½ ft), S: 60 cm (2 ft).

One of the very best yellow Floribundas, deservedly receiving plenty of publicity, It forms a neat, compact bush of shiny, light green leaves, studded with large, fragrant blooms. The urn-shaped flowers, with their slightly waved petals in a rich golden-yellow shade, deserve closer inspection. Excellent for cutting.

R. 'Lilac Charm'

Introduced in 1961.

H: 75 cm (2½ ft), S: 60 cm (2 ft).

This pale mauve rose is something of a rarity, for roses with this colouring are few and far between. It combines well with most colour schemes, from gentle pastels to the bold and brash.

R. 'Margaret Merril'

Introduced in 1977.

H: 75 cm (2½ ft), S: 75 cm (2½ ft).

An exquisite white, well-scented rose that has much more elegance than most Floribundas. The white buds, sometimes tinged with palest blush, open to reveal shapely flowers with a sweet, strong scent. An extremely versatile rose, it is equally happy in beds, borders and containers. An excellent Floribunda for cutting.

R. 'Mountbatten'

Introduced in 1982.

H: 1–1.5 m (3–5 ft), S: 80 cm (32 in).

This good, strong, yellow rose reaches a fine height for a Floribunda and will do well at the back of a border or in the middle of a bed to add height to a planting scheme. Neatly shaped buds open to full, rounded blooms in a fresh clear yellow. This robust, easy-to-grow rose is a real all-rounder – happy in beds and borders or grown as a hedge or a standard.

R. 'Queen Elizabeth'

Introduced in 1954, marking the accession of Queen Elizabeth II two years earlier.

H: 1.7 m (5½ ft), S: 90 cm (3 ft).

This pretty silvery-pink rose scores near maximum points on all counts, from cutting and colour to size and shape. Robust and easy to grow, it needs little attention save for a hard annual prune to maintain its neat form and to restrict its vigorous growth. As it is one of the taller Floribundas, it is an excellent choice for providing a backbone for a mixed border.

R. 'Sexy Rexy'

Introduced in 1984.

H: 75 cm (2½ ft), S: 60 cm (2 ft).

A prolific flowerer that is equally good in the garden and as a cut flower. The cool, strong pink of the flattish, camellia-like flowers contrasts well with the dark green leaves. A versatile beauty that is particularly attractive grown as a standard.

R. 'Trumpeter'

Introduced in 1977.

H: 60 cm (2 ft), S: 60 cm (2 ft).

This bushy rose produces generous clusters of vibrant, startling crimson blooms and makes a handsome addition to a small garden. It is largely trouble-free, and flowers reliably all through summer with no problems. Will thrive in many situations, from the back of the border to a container.

Above left: *R.* **'Sexy Rexy'**

Top right: *R.* **'Queen Elizabeth'**

Above right: *R.* **'Trumpeter'**

Far left: *R.* **'Korresia'**

Left: *R.* **'Margaret Merril'**

Opposite page: *R.* **'Mountbatten'**

The key difference between Climbers and Ramblers is that Climbers usually have long, stiff stems, whilst Ramblers have flexible, bendy shoots. Climbers are better suited to walls, whilst Ramblers are ideal for training over arches, pillars, pergolas and even up into trees.

climbers and ramblers

Climbers

There is always room for a climbing rose. They add a new, vertical dimension to the garden. You can grow them up against walls, into trees, over eyesores like garages, through hedges, and up pillars and posts. They change the scale of the garden.

There are an enormous number of Climbers to choose from. Smaller Climbers will reach about 1.8 m (6 ft), while some giants can spread up to 30 m (100 ft). Most of them scramble up walls, trees and shrubs by hooking their thorns over twigs and branches. They do need a leg-up – initial tying-in will send them safely on their way. Climbers that are not tied in create a very different effect, growing into wonderfully strange sprawling masses or arching mounds.

Climbers usually flower continuously throughout the summer months into autumn. Since their sturdy stems are leafless for four to five months of the year, exposing their support, you should grow them against something that is attractive to look at during the winter months. Wooden posts and stone walls or pillars are attractive in their own right or can be painted in bold and beautiful colours. If you feel creative, experiment with pieces of stained glass or broken china or tiles set into patches of concrete on a supporting wall.

Climbers are not a specific botanical group. Roses grouped in this category are usually repeat-flowering, large-flowered roses, and include Hybrid Teas, Noisettes and Floribundas. Strictly speaking, the Noisettes should be grouped with the Old garden roses, but I have included them in this section as the majority are repeat-flowering climbers. Be warned that these elegant roses can be slightly tender and to thrive they do need to be grown against a warm, sheltered wall.

Right top: **The large dark crimson flowers of 'Etoile de Holland' look stunning climbing against the white backdrop of a warm, sunny wall. The scent of this rose matches its vigour.**

Right centre: **The pink-flowering climber 'Madame Caroline Testout' gets high marks for repeat flowering, and with a really strong scent this rose would be an outright winner.**

Reds

There are a multitude of flamboyant red Climbers. The best reds begin with 'Etoile de Hollande, Climbing', which has a strong, rich scent and an abundance of rich crimson flowers, and has hardly been bettered since it first appeared back in 1931. It grows to a respectable 4.5 m (15 ft) high and adds to its main summer burst of flowers with a second flush in autumn. 'Crimson Glory, Climbing' is another red in the same league. It produces large, double, intensely fragrant crimson flowers in early summer, with more appearing later.

If you want an even darker red, try 'Guinée', a stunning, richly fragrant rose with deep wine-red flowers that are almost burgundy. It needs a bright, light background, as it will get lost set against red brick. The one drawback is that there is only one main flower show, in early summer, and after that just the occasional flowering. For brighter reds there is the reliable, all-summer-flowering 'Parkdirektor Riggers,' which reaches 3.7 m (12 ft). This is a bold, bright scarlet, and the only thing it lacks is scent, but the large clusters of flowers, with their wavy petals, are colourful and attractive enough for this not to matter.

Bold and glamorous, there are a multitude of flamboyant red Climbers.

Pinks

Left below: **No rose will ever excel against a north wall, but some, such as this 'Zéphirine Drouhin', do much better than others.**

Above left: **The bright red blooms of 'Parkdirektor Riggers' will flower all summer on a pergola.**

Above right: **'New Dawn' can be tied to a wall, but its loose, lax growth also looks fine tumbling over an arch.**

Pink Climbers have a soft 'cottage garden' aura and plenty of romantic appeal. 'Penny Lane' was the first climber to win the Rose of the Year award, in 1998. Carrying a mass of blush-pink flowers, it climbs 3.7 m (12 ft) high, and flowers for most of the summer. It looks wonderful teamed with 'Compassion', which has large, double, rounded flowers in a sumptuous shade of salmon-pink tinged with apricot, and a sensational scent. It is ideal for growing into old trees or through tall shrubs, like the silvery-grey *Elaeagnus* 'Quicksilver'. 'Caroline Testout, Climbing' is a gigantic pink, which can reach 6 m (20 ft) and practically cover the side of a house, its rich scent drifting through open windows. Even better, it tolerates less than perfect soil and a touch of shade.

'Souvenir de la Malmaison, Climbing' may only reach modest heights, about 3 m (10 ft), but it is a marvellous Bourbon, crammed with soft, silky, palest pink petals, and emitting a sweet,

spicy scent. It produces a first flush of flowers in summer, followed by an even better second show in early autumn. It is the perfect partner for the exquisite 'Zéphirine Drouhin' (another Bourbon), which has been a big favourite for 130 years, due to its cupped double flowers, in a delicious cerise shade, and sweet, rich fragrance. It will climb to 2.5 m (8 ft), and is perfect if you want to cover a north wall. 'Morning Jewel' is also useful, reaching 3 m (10 ft) and blanketing its support in clusters of clear pink flowers. It is robust and sturdy with good disease and weather resistance.

'New Dawn' is one of the most perfect Climbing pinks. It has been around now for nearly 70 years and reliably flowers all summer, producing pearly-pink, scented clusters. It is disease-free, and can flower over hedges or be grown as one itself, making a respectable 3 m (10 ft) screen. Grow it as a standard and it will droop dramatically, forming a mass of pink blooms.

Whites

'Mme Alfred Carrière' is an old Noisette climber, dating back to 1879, but is still one of the best. The double white flowers, tinged with palest pink, are set against pale green foliage and completely cover the 4.5 m (15 ft) of growth. Not only is this an exquisite beauty, it is also a thoroughly reliable, disease-free rose, with a sweet, delicate scent, that flowers happily into the autumn. Very hardy, this rose will tolerate a position against a north wall. 'Paul's Lemon Pillar' grows to about the same height, and has typical Hybrid Tea, high-pointed, shapely flowers. As the name suggests, it puts on a flamboyant display of enormous ivory flowers tinged with lemon, just before mid-summer. It is a marvellous sight, but the only drawback is that there is no repeat flowering. Even so, it is well worth growing.

The same can also be said of two shorter whites, 'Swan Lake' and 'White Cockade', both of which climb to about 2.5 m (8 ft), and are perfect for training up pillars. The former, its white flowers tinted with blush-pink, is a real beauty, flowering all summer, but is outdone by the latter, with its shapely, pure white flowers, delicate scent, neat growth and shiny dark green leaves. Both can be trained up T-shaped structures and look wonderful amongst massed plantings of blue or red.

Left: **The exquisite 'Swan Lake' should be grown up a pillar or post where its** shapely, pink-tinged white flowers can be enjoyed to the full.

Yellows

Yellow climbers have a rich, mellow charm, and look wonderful against weathered red brick or dark wood. 'Gloire de Dijon' is a buff-yellow Noisette rose with amber tints that has been very popular since the end of the Crimean War. Reaching 4.5 m (15 ft) , it is a gorgeous, repeat-flowering climber with a heavy scent. If you are a minimalist, plant it alone and enjoy its slightly bare, spare growth, otherwise mix it with another climber. 'Maigold' climbs to 3.7 m (12 ft) and is a vibrant yellow, highly scented Climber with plenty of glossy green leaves. It flowers profusely in early summer, before the other roses get going, but unfortunately will only flower spasmodically after the first flush. Not only does it put on a spectacular show, but it will also tolerate rather inhospitable conditions, such as poor soil and light shade.

There are four Climbing roses in the not-outrageously-large category. 'Golden Showers' reaches a very respectable 3 m (10 ft) and performs reliably for most of the summer. The clear yellow flowers are not particularly striking, but they do create a very pleasing massed effect and do not mind the shade of a north wall. If you have a warm, sheltered, south-facing wall, try 'Céline Forestier'. It is a 2.5 m (8 ft) high Noisette that needs a protected spot, but the delicate primrose-yellow flowers are wonderfully fragile and silky in appearance; they keep on coming, and the scent is heavenly. 'Leverkusen' is not quite so fussy, and gives a similar performance at a similar height, with a wonderful second show in the autumn. And 'Laura Ford' is a vigorous mini-climber as tall as a basketball player, with golden-yellow flowers borne on stiff stems that grow to 2 m (6½ ft) high.

Far left top: **The great 4.5 m (15 ft) high Noisette 'Alister Stella Gray', which dates back to 1894, provides a mass of flower sprays from mid-summer to mid-autumn.**

Left top: **If you need a Climber to flower in late spring, the orange-yellow 'Maigold' is a** good choice. This rose has a **strong scent and one main burst of flowers.**

Left bottom: **The pale yellow flowers of 'Leverkusen' enhance rather than conceal the mellow tone of this brick wall, and help lead the eye to the inner sanctum beyond.**

Ramblers

Ramblers are vigorous plants, shooting up through trellises, trees, arches and pergolas with enormous energy. With their long, bendy stems, they are ideal for training up, against and over garden structures. The majority of Ramblers do not repeat flower, but come into flower once a year, putting on a good display in early to mid-summer. However, repeat-flowering Ramblers are being raised. The small flowers can be double or semi-double and are massed in dense clusters. The choice of plants is huge, with a good colour range.

For genuine whites, there is a good choice of robust Ramblers.

Reds

The big two reds are 'Crimson Shower' and 'Paul's Scarlet Climber'. Both grow to approximately 4.5 m (15 ft) high. Train 'Crimson Shower' around a tree and it will be blanketed in deep crimson flowers for ten weeks from mid-summer. If that sounds a little garish, train it up a pergola among whites and blues and pinks to tone it down. Despite its name, 'Paul's Scarlet Climber' is listed as a Rambler. It produces a mass of rich scarlet flowers from early to mid-summer. Reliable and free-flowering, it will even tolerate poor, sandy soil and light shade.

Pinks

After 90 years, 'Debutante' is still one of the most popular Ramblers. It reaches 4.5 m (15 ft) and produces clear pink flowers with the gentlest, most subtle scent. 'Kew Rambler' is excellent for climbing up and around a tall stout tree. It produces 5.5 m (18 ft) stems clad in late-summer flowers. 'Paul's Himalayan Musk' grows even taller, sending out vigorous, long, twiggy growth, reaching up to 9 m (30 ft). It is at its best in mid-summer, when for about two weeks it will cover even the tallest hedge or trees in a cloak of palest pink. At night, under a full moon, it is like finding a strange new gleaming white wall in the garden.

Above: **If you have a tree that needs a late summer show, grow a 'Kew Rambler' into it. As the name suggests, it was raised at Kew, in 1912.**

Left: **The 2.2 m (7 ft) high pink shrub rose 'Constance Spry' is paired with a 'Rambling Rector', which in full cry can reach a height of 6 m (20 ft) with a coiling mass of white flowers. It can be sent either shooting through shrubs and trees, or over anything from walls to sheds.**

Right: **Here two well-scented Ramblers have joined forces – the rampant white 'Wedding Day' and the much shorter, yellow 'Goldfinch.'**

Whites

For genuine whites there is an excellent choice of robust Ramblers. The flowers of 'Wedding Day' open as a rich yellow shade, but soon turn to creamy-white. It scrambles to 8 m (26 ft) high, producing flattish, single flowers through the second half of summer. The sweet, fruity scent is quite delicious. 'Sir Cedric Morris' grows just as high, and also produces a concentrated burst of flowers in mid-summer. So too does 'Albéric Barbier', whose abundance of small yellow buds open to reveal papery white flowers highlighted by glossy, dark green foliage. The flowers have a fragile charm that more than makes up for the lack of scent. At 6 m (20 ft), 'Seagull' is shorter, but it is still one of the best roses for growing up old trees. The flat, single or semi-double white flowers are enlivened by rich golden stamens, and the overall effect of the clustered flowers is reminiscent of fluffed-up blossom. 'Bobbie James' has similar flowers but it is fractionally more vigorous, growing to 9 m (30 ft), its strong thorns quickly anchoring it to a tree. The scent is big, the leaves shiny and the whole effect hugely impressive.

Slightly shorter white Ramblers include 'Rambling Rector', which reaches 6 m (20 ft) and puts on a wonderful display in mid-summer. It can be used to grow against anything – allow it to sprint up and around old apple trees or to scramble over less-than-beautiful garden structures. A vigorous and robust Rambler, it will even tolerate shady walls. 'Félicité Perpétue' is another excellent, reliable Rambler for shadier spots or poor soil. It gives a remarkable mid-summer show, producing a profusion of sweetly scented creamy-white blooms. This rose never disappoints, and is cheerfully, remorselessly healthy. 'The Garland' is perfect for 4.5 m (15 ft) high pillars. It combines a wonderful, strong scent with generous swags of salmon-pink flowers in mid-summer, and for that alone deserves a corner in every garden.

climbers and ramblers gallery

R. 'Albertine' (Rambler)

Introduced in 1921.

Grows to 5 m (16 ft).

A bushy Rambler with arching, thorny stems that carry small clusters of peach-pink, almost coppery, cupped double blooms. It flowers for a few weeks in mid-summer. Without a support, it will form a sprawling, mounded shrub.

R. 'Compassion' (Climber)

Introduced in 1973.

Grows to 3 m (10 ft).

A stiff, sturdy Climber best suited to training up against a strong wall. The stylish, shapely flowers are luscious pink with a dash of apricot and a strong, delicious scent. Grow where the flowers can be seen close up.

R. 'Crimson Shower' (Rambler)

Introduced in 1951.

Grows to 4.5 m (15 ft).

This is an excellent choice for a vibrant blast of red in the garden. Unlike other Ramblers, which flower once around mid-summer, this blooms from summer until early autumn. The small clustered flowers are a deep rich crimson, with a delicious, honeyed scent.

R. 'Etoile de Hollande, Climbing' (Climber)

Introduced in 1931.

Grows to 4.5 m (15 ft).

This popular rose combines rich red colouring with a rich strong scent. Individually the flowers are unspectacular, but they make up for this with the richness and abundance of their display.

R. 'Maigold' (Climber)

Introduced in 1953.

Grows to 3.7 m (12 ft).

A consistently popular rich golden-yellow climber with attractive, shiny foliage that flowers before its rivals in early summer. Some blooms appear thereafter, but not many. This tough, hardy and disease-resistant rose will withstand less-than-perfect conditions, and is happy in poor soil and light shade. Excellent for exposed sites.

R. 'Mme Alfred Carrière' (Climber)

Introduced in 1879.

Grows to 4.5 m (15 ft), but with pruning can be kept as a shrub about half that height.

A well-loved Noisette rose with plenty of old-fashioned charm. The milky-white to pale pink flowers are fragrant and rounded. A reliable rose that will grow against north walls and puts on a long summer display.

R. 'New Dawn' (Rambler)

Introduced in 1930.

Grows to 3 m (10 ft).

An excellent, all-purpose, pearly-pink Rambler with a long flowering season and strong sweet scent. It is easy to train up against an arch, pillar or pergola.

R. 'Paul's Scarlet Climber' (Climber/Rambler)

Introduced in 1915.

Grows to 3 m (10 ft).

A reliable, vigorous rose producing numerous shoots from the base. The vivid scarlet flowers are carried in clusters. Prone to mildew in dry sites.

R. 'Pink Perpétué' (Climber)

Introduced in 1965.

Grows to 3 m (10 ft).

A clear pink rose with large flowers and light scent that repeat flowers throughout the summer and autumn.

R. 'Seagull' (Rambler)

Introduced in 1907.

Grows to 6 m (20 ft).

The abundant, small, single to semi-double white flowers with golden stamens are carried on long arching stems. Excellent grown through a tree.

R. 'Zéphirine Drouhin' (Climber)

Introduced in 1868.

Grows to 3 m (10 ft).

Around for over a hundred years and still a terrific rose, this sweetly scented beauty repeat flowers throughout summer and autumn, producing rich pink blooms.

Right: *R.* **'New Dawn'**

Far right: *R.* **'Paul's Scarlet Climber'**

Below left: *R.* **'Maigold'**

Below centre: *R.* **'Compassion'**

Below right: *R.* **'Zéphirine Drouhln'**

Bottom left: *R.* **'Mme Alfred Carrière'**

Bottom centre: *R.* **'Albertine'**

Bottom right: *R.* **'Seagull'**

Opposite page: *R.* **'Pink Perpétué'**

Miniature roses are tiny versions of Large- and Cluster-flowered bush roses. Repeat flowering, they can be grown in beds and borders, but are at their happiest in pots. Patio roses were originally known as Dwarf cluster-flowered bush roses, as they are a smaller version of this group.

miniature and patio

Miniature roses

Miniature roses were extremely fashionable in the early and mid-19th century, when they were grown in pots as tiny specimen plants, but towards the end of the century they fell out of favour, and by the end of the century they had virtually disappeared. Then, in 1918, a Dr. Roulet saw some Miniatures growing in pots in Switzerland. They became known as 'Rouleti', and, under this name, the Miniatures were relaunched in Europe.

Miniature roses are now making a comeback. They are hugely popular in America, thanks largely to the endeavours of one Californian breeder, Ralph Moore. Hundreds of new varieties have been bred, with twiggy stems and tiny flowers and foliage, although their scent is generally slight. They are usually about 30 cm (12 in) high and, as they are sold in pots, many people make the mistake of thinking they are houseplants. In fact,

Miniatures are quite hardy and will not survive for long in a dry, warm, indoor atmosphere. They flower from mid-summer into autumn, eventually being zapped by the cold. Minatures can be grown anywhere – in containers, in gaps in paving, lining paths, around ponds, in windowboxes, tubs and terracotta pots.

'Stars 'n' Stripes' is a fun Californian, producing white flowers with red stripes and yellow stamens. If it is too gaudy for your taste, there are many others to choose from. 'Starina' is a gorgeous shapely red that goes well with 'Rise 'n' Shine', which has high-pointed buds in egg-yolk yellow. 'Robin Redbreast', sometimes listed as a Ground-cover rose, has exquisite, eye-catching red flowers set against glossy foliage. 'Angela Rippon' and 'Stacey Sue' are deep, luscious pinks, 'Easter Morning' a pure ivory-white, and 'Red Sunblaze' a gorgeous deep red.

Above: **The Miniature 'Starina' keeps flowering from early summer to within eight weeks of Christmas. Like other tiny, scaled-down roses, it can be grown in pots or at the front of the border.**

Above right: **The peach-apricot flowers of the Patio rose 'Sweet Dream' are accompanied by plenty of glossy foliage.**

Right: **The bright red, velvety flowers of the 45 cm (18 in) high Patio rose 'Festival' make a colourful splash in a summer border.**

Patio roses

Patio roses have become very popular despite their lack of scent, especially with the recent emphasis on stylish small gardens. Originally known as Dwarf Floribundas, they were first listed as Patio roses in 1984. They are a cross between the Miniatures and the Cluster-flowered bush roses (or Floribundas), and are just about half-way between the two in size.

Small and neat in habit, two of the best are 'Sweet Dream' and 'Top Marks'. The former is the UK's best-selling Patio rose. It has peachy-apricot cupped blooms, held in clusters and combined with glossy leaves. The latter rose has dense clusters of long-lasting orange-vermilion flowers. 'Shine On' is a rich apricot tinged with salmon-pink, 'Perestroika' a bright zingy yellow, and 'Gentle Touch' a fabulous little pale pink with golden stamens. 'Festival' is a wonderfully unusual bright red with velvety double blooms and glossy, dark green leaves.

Climbing Miniatures

Climbing Miniatures grow to a height of 2.2–2.7 m (7–9 ft), the miniature feature being the foliage and flowers rather than the stems. They flower from early summer to the first frosts, creating vertical columns of colour. Climbing Miniatures first went on sale in the UK in 1990. The first available was the golden-yellow 'Laura Ford' (available in America under the name 'King Tut'), which is a cross between the Patio rose 'Anna Ford' and an unnamed seedling climber.

Climbing Miniatures are still very new, and only a handful are available as yet. From the limited selection on offer, two of the best are 'Nice Day', a pretty salmon pink, and 'Warm Welcome', a striking, glowing orange-scarlet shade. Climbing Miniatures can be pruned to restrict their height, but the plants will then send out more climbing shoots from the base, making the rose much bushier. In other words, it is best to leave well alone. Rose breeders are now working towards producing more arching Miniature Ramblers.

miniature and patio gallery

R. 'Angela Rippon' (Miniature)

Introduced in 1978.

Grows to 35 cm (14 in) high.

A rich deep pink Miniature rose bearing flattish double flowers. Repeat flowers throughout summer and autumn. Excellent planted around a white plinth or the foot of a pergola.

R. 'Anna Ford' (Patio)

Introduced in 1981.

Grows to 45 cm (18 in) high.

A bushy, low Patio rose with an abundance of small, dark, glossy leaves. The orange-red, semi-double flowers open flat, revealing a golden centre. Good for low hedging.

R. 'Easter Morning' (Miniature)

Introduced in 1960.

Grows to 30 cm (12 in) high.

Multi-petalled, ivory-white flowers make this dainty Miniature really stand out. Ideal in a mixed border – try planting several bushes and allowing them to run through the border, threading in loops and scroll-like patterns through the other plants. The small, creamy flowers look particularly charming teamed with blues and greens.

R. 'Festival' (Patio)

Introduced in 1994.

Grows to 60 cm (2 ft) high.

This recent addition to the Patio roses available is a compact rose with a neat habit that forms a tidy, dense bush. The flowers are rich crimson in colour, crammed with velvety petals and with a light scent. It can be squeezed into small spaces; alternatively, it looks wonderful grown as a standard.

R. 'Gentle Touch' (Patio)

Introduced in 1986.

Grows to 45 cm (18 in) high.

Shapely buds open to reveal small, elegant flowers in a delicate pale pink tinged with apricot, highlighted by glossy dark green leaves. It even has a light, sweet, delicate scent. Excellent in a container, where the flowers can be appreciated. It is easy to see why this is a best-seller.

R. 'Laura Ford' (Climbing Miniature)

Introduced in 1990.

Grows to 2.2 m (7 ft) high.

A good pillar rose for the back of the border, its golden-yellow flowers appearing from summer to autumn and mixing well with whites and ornamental wispy grasses. Also excellent trained against a low wall or fence.

R. 'Rise 'n' Shine' (Miniature)

Introduced in 1977.

Grows to 40 cm (16 in) high.

The buds open to reveal relatively large flowers with pointed petals in bright yellow that are almost scentless. The bushy, upright plants are good for borders or low hedging.

R. 'Shine On' (Patio)

Introduced in 1994.

Grows to 40 cm (16 in) high.

A small, compact bush carrying clusters of shapely flowers crammed with satiny petals in an eye-catching orange shade. The densely massed blooms have a light, delicate fragrance and are good for cutting, containers or bedding schemes.

R. 'Stars 'n' Stripes' (Miniature)

Introduced in 1975.

Grows to 40 cm (16 in) high.

A bright and cheerful Miniature rose, although its red-and-white striped flowers with their golden stamens may be a little too brash for some tastes.

R. 'Sweet Dream' (Patio)

Introduced in 1988.

Grows to 50 cm (20 in) high.

This Patio rose produces shapely flowers in a peachy-apricot hue carried on a bushy, upright plant. Unlike many Patio roses, it has a light scent.

R. 'Top Marks' (Patio)

Introduced in 1992.

Grows to 40 cm (16 in) high.

Shapely flowers in a bright orange tinged with vermilion are carried in dense clusters above small glossy leaves.

Above left: *R.* **'Angela Rippon'**

Top right: *R.* **'Festival'**

Above right: *R.* **'Gentle Touch'**

Far left: *R.* **'Sweet Dream'**

Left: *R.* **'Top Marks'**

Opposite page: *R.* **'Anna Ford'**

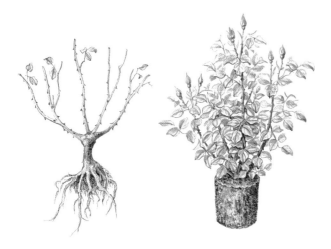

Buying a bare-root rose Look for a good network of fibrous roots and a strong bud union. Reject any that have been allowed to dry out, and plant as soon as possible after purchase.

Buying a container-grown rose Make sure that plants have sturdy, healthy, well-balanced stems and vigorous foliage of a good colour. Check that the compost is moist.

Planting a bare-root rose Place the rose in the centre of a prepared hole. Use a cane to check that the bud union will be 2.5 cm (1¼ in) below soil level.

Planting a hedge with bush roses Planting two rows, about 45–60 cm (1½–2 ft) apart, in a staggered formation will result in a denser hedge.

care and cultivation

Choosing roses

Roses can be bought either bare-rooted or container-grown. Bare-root roses have been dug up from growing fields and are in a dormant state. Their roots are bare of soil, but are sometimes packed in peat or compost. When buying mail-order roses from specialist suppliers, who always offer a broader and more imaginative range than garden centres, this is invariably how they are delivered. For the best results, bare-root roses should be planted in late autumn, but they can also be planted in winter, as long as the ground is not waterlogged or frozen.

Container-grown roses (i.e. those bought from garden centres) can be planted at any time of year, even during the summer, except during a period of drought or when the ground is frozen. All the books recommend that you reject any plants with a congested or pot-bound root system. In reality, you cannot walk round a garden centre taking them all out of their pots. However, you can avoid plants with feeble, twiggy growth, dead wood or spindly shoots. Look for sturdy, healthy, well-balanced stems and sound foliage. A climbing rose should have 60–75 cm (2–2½ ft) long stems. Standard roses should have a nicely rounded head and a sturdy stem.

Planting roses

When choosing a planting spot, bear in mind that most roses thrive in full sun in humus-rich, fertile soil with good drainage. Roses require good air circulation but need to be kept away from strong winds. Avoid planting in deep shade, especially under trees.

Bare-root roses

Plant in late autumn or early winter. If the plants are dry, soak the roots in a bucket of water for a couple of hours. Then prune away any damaged or dead wood, to create an attractive, open shape. Plant the roses as soon as possible, unless conditions are adverse. If delays do occur, keep the roses cool and frost-free, occasionally standing the roots in a bucket of water to prevent them from drying out. Dig a planting hole and add half a bucket of organic matter and a handful of bonemeal. Place the rose in the planting hole, positioning it so that the bud union is about 2.5 cm (1¼ in) below soil level. Fan out the roots so they can grow in their natural direction. Half fill in the hole with soil, tread it down well so there are no air pockets, then fill in the remainder of the hole. Finally, firm down the surrounding soil gently, and then water generously.

Container roses

Before planting, submerge the pot in a bucket of water until the compost is saturated. Dig the planting hole, wetting the ground if it is dry. Add garden compost and a sprinkling of bonemeal to the bottom of the hole. Invert the container and slide out the rose. Place it in the hole and tease out the roots to fan in all directions. Fill in the hole around the plant with a mix of good soil, peat and a sprinkling of bonemeal. Make sure the soil level is flush with the surrounding ground, then water in well. For a standard rose, place a stake in a corner of the planting hole and place the plant against it, allowing the roots a free run.

Climbers

For wall-grown climbers it is necessary first to attach wire supports for the rose to climb against. Drill vine eyes into the wall (or to battens that can then be attached to the wall) at 40 cm (16 in) intervals. Run lengths of strong, galvanized wire through the vine eyes. Keep the wire about 8 cm (3 in) away from the surface for good air circulation. Dig the planting hole approximately 30–45 cm (12–18 in) away from the generally dry, impoverished ground at the base of the wall. Place the rose in the hole at a 45° angle, leaning towards the lowest support wire, and fan out the roots in the direction of the open garden. Train the stems along canes to guide them towards the wall. Water in generously. Climbers growing into trees and hedges should be planted about 90 cm (3 ft) away from the plant. Make sure they are positioned so that the stems will be blown towards rather than away from the tree. Tie in until the rose has grown big enough to latch its thorns onto the branches.

Rose hedges

Plant tall, spreading roses about 90 cm (3 ft) apart in a single line so that the branches of mature plants will intermingle. Plant shorter, more upright roses in two rows, about 45–60 cm (1½–2 ft) apart, in a staggered formation.

Routine care
Feeding

Roses are gross feeders, and if they are to perform well they will benefit greatly from a mulch of compost or manure, and/or a proprietary rose feed in spring, and again in mid-summer.

Dead-heading

For a long flower display, regular dead-heading is vital. It diverts the plant's energy from making seeds to producing new flower buds. Cut off dead-heads just above the second leaf joint below the spent flower. Do not dead-head those roses that produce a good display of rose hips, or flower only once. Autumn dead-heading is not required.

Suckers

These fast-growing stems are produced from below the bud union, and grow from ground level. They usually have slightly different foliage, similar to a wild rose, and drain the rose's energy. Suckers should be promptly removed by tearing them off from the rootstock with a sharp twist. Do not cut the sucker as this will stimulate dormant sucker buds to grow.

Pruning

The purpose of pruning is to prompt the growth of vigorous new stems by removing older, tired and dead wood. It also helps to maintain a good shape. Roses should usually be pruned in winter or early spring. Do not prune in very cold weather as frost may damage new growth. Use sharp secateurs and make a clean cut. Pruning cuts should be made about 5 mm (¼ in) above an outward-facing bud. Angle the cut so that rain will run away from the new bud. Each rose group has slightly different pruning requirements. All, though, save standards and climbers, should be pruned hard on planting to prompt new growth from the base, instead of higher up the stems. Pruning can seem complicated, but do not worry too much. Roses always survive.

Dead-heading With a pair of secateurs, cut off dead-heads just above the second leaf joint below the spent flower.

Removing suckers Do not cut them off at ground level, but scrape away the soil around the rose to reveal the top of the rootstock and tear the sucker off with a sharp twist.

Making a pruning cut Cut at an angle, about 5 mm (¼ in) above an outward-facing bud, with the bud near the top of the cut. Do not cut too far away from the bud as this can cause disease to enter the stem. Always cut back into healthy white wood.

Pruning a Species rose Remove dead and diseased wood, and thin out any dense or congested stems.

Pruning a Climber In the first two years after planting, simply remove any dead or diseased wood. From the third year, prune in autumn after flowering.

Pruning a Cluster-flowered bush rose Remove spent flower heads with a pair of secateurs. This encourages new flowers to develop and helps to strengthen the roots.

Pruning a Large-flowered bush rose Remove any dead, damaged or crossing branches and cut back the remaining stems to within 20–25 cm (8–10 in) of ground level.

Species roses

After the initial planting prune, which creates a sound framework, little is required beyond general maintenance. Removing dead and diseased wood promptly should ensure that they bloom freely for many years. Species roses can be thinned out if they become too dense and congested. Periodically, vigorous new stems appear from the base to replace the old, which should be cut away.

Old roses

Single-flush flowering old roses
Old roses such as Damasks, Albas and Gallicas flower on old wood so they should be pruned soon after flowering. Prune the main growth by about one-third, and side shoots by two-thirds. Gallicas can quickly become congested with twiggy growth, so this should be regularly cut back by about two-thirds in late summer to improve air circulation.

Repeat-flowering old roses
These roses include Bourbons, Chinas, Portlands and Hybrid Perpetuals and should be pruned in late winter or early spring. Cut back side shoots and prune vigorous new stems by about one-third of their length. Cut back weaker stems even harder, to force strong new shoots. The aim is to create an attractive framework of strong, vigorous stems. In addition, repeat-flowering old roses need a light prune after flowering in order to remove twiggy or spindly side growth. China roses need to have only their weaker stems cut back.

Modern shrub roses

Modern shrub roses should be pruned when dormant, in early spring. Light pruning produces a larger plant with more flowers. Harder pruning reduces the overall size of the bush, which will then produce fewer quality blooms. It is important to remember to prune always to an outward-facing bud.

Pruning a Rambler Prune in late summer after flowering. Ramblers can become tangled and choked with excess growth if left unpruned.

Pruning a miniature Cut out twiggy growth, and reduce main stems by half.

Large-flowered bush roses (Hybrid Teas)

These should be pruned quite hard in early spring. Remove all damaged, diseased or dead wood and chop off any unproductive shoots. Remove stems that cross other growth to produce a well-balanced framework and improve air circulation. Cut back the remaining stems to within 20–25 cm (8–10 in) off the ground.

Cluster-flowered bush roses (Floribundas)

Cluster-flowered bush roses need a less severe annual pruning than the Large-flowered bush roses. Prune in early spring, cutting away any unproductive wood and removing dead, diseased and damaged growth. Reduce any side shoots by one- to two-thirds, and prune the remaining stems to between 25–45 cm (10–18 in) from the ground. Less vigorous shoots should be cut back more severely, to stimulate growth.

Climbers

Unlike most roses, climbers should not be pruned when planted, especially if their name includes the word 'Climbing', except to remove dead wood. Build up an attractive shape by tying in the stems horizontally as soon as they reach the lowest level of the supports. For the first two years, Climbers need only have dead and diseased wood removed. From the third year on, they should be pruned in autumn, after flowering. Prune main shoots to keep them within the desired area and cut short side shoots back by two-thirds. The aim is to cover as wide an area as possible low down to avoid too bare a leg. If the base of an established climber looks bare, cut back the oldest flowering stems to a height of 30 cm (12 in).

Ramblers

Ramblers should be pruned hard on planting to ensure vigorous growth. Unlike climbers, they rarely have bare legs – in fact excessively thick growth at the base is more likely. If left unpruned, ramblers can become tangled and choked with excess growth. They should be cut back in late summer, after flowering. For the first two years, side shoots should be trimmed to a vigorous shoot. From the third year on, about one-third of the oldest flowering shoots must be cut back to the base of the plant. Fill any gaps in the framework by tying in new shoots. Hugely tangled, choked ramblers needing renovation can be cut right back. They will quickly recover.

Miniatures

Cut out twiggy growth, and reduce main stems by a half of their length.

Standards

Standard roses are usually bought ready trained. Once established, prune to keep the top-growth from becoming top-heavy and to maintain an attractive round shape.

Pests and diseases

Avoid planting new roses in beds where roses have been grown before – they tend to succumb to 'rose-sickness' or 'replant disease', and rarely succeed. Roses are also prone to various pests and diseases, the most common being:

Black spot
A common fungal disease that disfigures leaves. Destroy affected leaves and treat the plant with a fungicide spray.

Canker
Canker results in discoloured and dying stems. Prune the affected tissue, cutting back to healthy wood.

Rust
Another fungal disease, this produces unsightly orange spots on the underside of the leaves. Remove all infected stems and spray with a fungicide.

Index

Figures in italics refer to captions.

air circulation, 74, 75, 76, 77
arches, 29, 59, *61*, 64, 66

banks, 37
bare-root roses, 74, *74*
battens, 75
birds, 20
black spot, 77
bonemeal, 74

canes, 75
canker, 77
China, *18*, 44
coastal areas, 17, 40
compost, 38, 74, *74*, 75
container-grown roses, 74, *74*
containers, 56, 70, 72
cottage gardens, 10, 56, 61
courtyards, *36*
cut flowers, *27*, 35, 38, 40, 45, 48, 52, 53, 56, 72

dead-heading, 20, 48, 56, 75, *75*
disease resistance, 7–8
diseases, 77
drainage, 48, 74

feeding, 75
fences, 72
formal gardens, *8*, 11, 14, 37
fungicides, 77

garden centres, 7, 74
genetic breeding, 8
gravel, *39*

hedging, *7*, 10, 11, 14, 15, 17, *17*, *18*, 20, 24, 28, 30, 34, 38, 39, 40, 48, 55, 56, 60, 61, 64, 72, *74*, 75
herb gardens, 37
humus, 27, 29, 38, 48, 74

island beds, 11, *54*

lawns, 39

manure, 75
mildew, 52, 66
mulch, 75

organic matter, 74

paths, 11, *17*, 70
paving, 70
peat, 74
pergolas, 16, 59, *61*, 64, 66, 72
pesticides, 8
pests, 77
pillars, 59, 60, 62, *62*, 65, 66, 72
planting roses, 74–5, *74*
ponds, 11, 70
posts, 60, *62*
pots, 70, *70*, 74
pruning, 14, *17*, *18*, 20, 24, 26, 39, 56, 74, 75–6, *75*, *76*

raised beds, *52*
remontant roses, 10
'replant disease', 77
rose breeding, 6–8
rose classification, 10–11
rose-sickness, 77
rust, 77

sand, 14, 17, 64
shade, 10, 24, 40, 61, 63–6, 74
sheds, *64*
small gardens, 15, 39
soils
   fertile, 26, 27, 29, 56, 74
   humus-rich, 48, 74
   less-fertile, 40, 61
   moist, 40, 56
   poor, 29, 63–6, 75
   sandy, 17, 64
staking, 74
suckers, *18*, 28, 75, *75*
support, *24*, 26, 30, 66, 75

thickets, 14, 15, *18*, 20
training, 29, 75
trees, 10, 15, *15*, 16, 20, 36, 60, 61, 64, *64*, 65, 66, 74, 75
trellises, 30, 64
tubs, 70
tying in, 29, 60, *61*

vine eyes, 75

walled gardens, *15*
walls, 37, 40, 60, *64*, 75
   brick, 16, 61, *63*
   low, 72
   north, 61, *61*, 63, 66
   shady, 65
   south-facing, 16, 63
   stone, 60
   warm, 60, *60*, 63
windowboxes, 70
wire supports, 75

Plant index

Figures in italics refer to captions.

achilleas, *7*
Alba roses, 10, 24, *24*, 30, 76
'Albéric Barbier', 65
'Albertine', 66, *67*
alchemilla, 45
Alchemilla mollis, *39*
'Alec's Red', 45, *45*
'Alister Stella Gray', *63*
'Angela Rippon', 70, 72, *73*
'Anna Ford', 71, 72, *73*
Apothecary's Rose, 6, 28, 30
apple trees, 15
'Apricot Nectar', 54, 56
'Assemblage des Beautés', 28

'Ballerina', 38, *39*
banksiae var. *banksiae*, 16, *17*, 20
banksiae 'Lutea', 16, 20, *21*
Banksian Roses, 16, 20
'Baron Girod de l'Ain', 29
'Baronne Prévost', 29
'Beautiful Britain', 52
'Belle de Crécy', 28, 30, *31*
bergenias, *7*
'Blanche Double de Coubert', 39, 40, *41*
'Bobbie James', 65
'Boule de Neige', 25
Bourbon roses, 7, 24, *24*, 25, 30, 61, 76
box, 11

'Brother Cadfael', 35
brunonii, 15
   'La Mortola', 15, 20
'Buff Beauty', *7*, 38, *39*, 40, *41*
bush roses, 11

'Capitaine John Ingram', 29
'Cardinal de Richelieu', 28
'Céleste' (Celestial), 24, 30, *31*
'Céline Forestier', 63
'Celsiana', 27
× *centifolia*, 26, *26*, 27
   'Muscosa', 29
Centifolia roses, 24, 26, *26*, 29
'Cerise Bouquet', *36*, 37
'Chanelle', 53
'Charles de Mills', 28
China roses, 6, 7, 24, 25, 26, 76
'City of London', 53
Clematis 'Countess of Lovelace', *7*
Climbers, 8, 10, 11, 14, 15, *15*, 16, 20, 36, 38, 59, 60–63, 66, *67*, 74, 75, *76*, 77
Climbing Miniatures, 11, 71, 72
Cluster-flowered bush roses (Floribundas), 11, 36, 38, 43, 50–57, 60, 69, 71, *76*, 77
Cluster-flowered Polyantha roses, 51, 52
'Commandant Beaurepaire', 25, 30
'Compassion', 61, 66, *67*
'Complicata', 28
'Comte de Chambord', *29*
'Comtesse de Murinais', 29
'Constance Spry', *64*
copper beech, 15
'Cornelia', 38
'Crimson Glory, Climbing', 61
'Crimson Shower', 64, 66

damascena var. *semperflorens*, 27
Damask roses, 7, 24, 25, 27, *27*, 30, 76
'De Meaux', 26
'Debutante', 64
delphiniums, 37, *44*, 45
'Duchesse de Montebello', 28

'Dupontii', 37
'Dutch Gold', 47
Dwarf Cluster-flowered bush roses, 69
Dwarf Floribundas, 71

'Easter Morning', 70, 72
eglanteria, 17
Elaeagnus 'Quicksilver', 61
'Elina', 47, 48, *49*
'Elizabeth Harkness', 46, 48
'Else Poulsen', 52, *52*
'Ena Harkness', 45, 48
'English Miss', 53, *53*
English roses, 10, 33, 35, *35*, 40
'Etoile de Holland, Climbing', *60*, 61, 66
'Europeana', 52
'Evening Star', 47

'Fantin-Latour', 26
'Félicité Parmentier', 24
'Félicité Perpétué', 65
'Festival', *70*, 71, 72, *73*
filipes 'Kiftsgate', 10, 15, *15*
'Five-coloured China Rose', 26
Floribundas *see* Cluster-flowered bush roses
foetida 'Persiana', *7*
forrestiana, 17
'Fragrant Cloud', 45, *45*
'Fragrant Delight', 54, *54*
'Freedom', 47
'Fritz Nobis', 10, 36
'Fru Dagmar Hastrup', *17*
'Frühlingsgold', 37, 40, *41*
'Frühlingsmorgen', 36

gallica var. *officinalis*, 28, 30, *31*
Gallica roses, 6, 10, 24, 28, *28*, 30, 76
'Gentle Touch', 71, 72, *73*
'Georg Arends', 29
'Geranium', 14, 18
geraniums, 45
'Gertrude Jekyll', *11*, 35, 37, 40, *41*
'Glamis Castle', 35
glauca, 17–18, *17*, 20, *21*

'Gloire de Dijon', 63
'Gloire de France', 28
'Golden Showers', 63
'Golden Wedding', 55, 56
'Golden Wings', 37, 40, *41*
'Goldfinch', *64*
'Graham Thomas', 35, *35*, 40,
    41
grasses, 45, 72
'Great Maiden's Blush', 24
'Great Ormond Street', 55
Ground-cover roses, 10–11, 14,
    15, 16, 20, 37, *37*
'Guinée', 61

helenae, 15, *15*, 20, *21*
hemerocallis, *7*
'Henri Martin', 29, 30, *31*
'Henry Kelsey', 37
herbs, 45
'Heritage', 35
'Hermosa', 26
Himalayan Musk, 15
hops, *7*
Hybrid Musks, 11, 33, 36, 38,
    39, 40
Hybrid Perpetual roses, 24, 29,
    44, 76
Hybrid Teas *see* Large-
    flowered bush roses

'Ice Cream', 47
'Iceberg', *54*, 55
'Indigo', 29, 30
'Ispahan', 27, *27*, 30, *31*

'Jacqueline du Pré', *7*, 37, 40,
    41
'Just Joey', 46, *46*

'Kew Rambler', 64, *64*
'King Tut', 71
'Kirsten Poulsen', 52
'Königin von Dänemark'
    ('Queen of Denmark'),
    24, *24*
'Korresia', 55, 56, *57*

'L. D. Braithwaite', 35, *35*, 40
'La France', 44

'La Ville de Bruxelles', 27
laburnum, *36*
'Lady Curzon', 36
'Lady Hillingdon', 29
Large-flowered bush roses
    (Hybrid Teas), 11, 36, 42–9,
    51, 52, 60, 62, 69, *76*, 77
'Laura Ford', 63, 71, 72
lavenders, 45
'Leverkusen', 63, *63*
'Lilac Charm', 54, 56
'Lilian Austin', 35
'Little White Pet', 37
longicuspis var. *sinowilsonii*, 16
'Louise Odier', *24*, 25
'Lovely Lady', 46, *46*
'Loving Memory', 45
Lychnis coronaria, 27

macrophylla, 18
'Magic Carpet', 37
'Maigold', 63, *63*, 66, *67*
'Marchesa Boccella', 29
'Maréchal Davoust', 29
'Margaret Merril', 55, 56, *57*
'Marguerite Hilling', 36
'Marie Louise', 10, 27
'Marjorie Fair', 38
'Max Graf', 10, 37
'Melody Maker', 52
miniature climbers *see*
    Climbing Miniatures
Miniature Ramblers, 71
Miniature roses, 11, 69, 70, *70*,
    72, *73*, 77, *77*
'Mme Alfred Carrière', 62, 66,
    67
'Mme Caroline Testout,
    Climbing', *60*, 61
'Mme Hardy', 27, 30
'Mme Isaac Pereire', 10, *24*, 25,
    30, *31*
'Mme Knorr', 29, *29*
'Mme Legras de St. Germain',
    24
Modern bush roses, 34, 43, *74*
Modern garden roses, 10–11
Modern shrub roses, 10, 32–41,
    76
monardas, *7*

moschata, 16
'Morning Jewel', 61
Moss roses, 10, 24, 29, 30
'Mountbatten', 55, 56, *57*
moyesii, 14, 18, *18*, 20, *21*
'Mrs Anthony Waterer', 37
'Mrs Doreen Pike', 39
'Mrs John Laing', 29
mulliganii, 15
multibracteata, 18
multiflora, 15
Musk rose, 7, 38
'My Joy', 46

'Nevada', *36*, 37, 40, *41*
'New Dawn', 61, *61*, 66, *67*
'New Zealand', 46
'News', 54
'Nice Day', 71
nicotianas, *11*
Noisette roses, 7, 10, 60, 62,
    63, *63*, 66
'Nozomi', 37

× *odorata* 'Mutabilis', 7, 26,
    30, *31*
'Old Blush', 25, 26
Old garden roses, *7*, 10, 22–31,
    60, 76
'Oranges and Lemons', 54

'Parkdirektor Riggers', 61, *61*
Patio roses, 11, 69, *70*, 71, 72, *73*
'Paul's Himalayan Musk', 64
'Paul's Lemon Pillar', 62
'Paul's Scarlet Climber', 64,
    66, *67*
'Peace', 11, 47, *47*, 48, *49*
'Peaudouce', 47
pelargoniums, *11*
'Penelope', 38
'Penny Lane', 61
'Perestroika', 71
'Petite de Hollande', 26
petunias, *11*
phormium, *52*
pimpinellifolia, 18, *18*
'Pink Parfait', 53, *53*
'Pink Perpétué', 66, *67*
'Pleine de Grâce', 37

'Polar Star', 47, 48, *49*
Portland roses, 24, 29, *29*, 30, 76
'Président de Sèze', 28, 30, *31*
'Pristine', 47
pulverulenta, 18

'Quatre Saisons', 27
'Queen Elizabeth', 53, 56, *57*

Ramblers, 11, *15*, 16, 20, 59,
    64–5, 66, *67*, 77, *77*
'Rambling Rector', *64*, 65
'Raubritter', 37, *37*
'Red Sunblaze', 70
'Reine des Violettes', 29
'Reine Victoria', *7*, 25
'Remember Me', 46, 48, *49*
'René d'Anjou', 29
'Rise 'n' Shine', 70, 72
'Robert le Diable', 26, 30
'Robin Redbreast', 70
Rose of Lancaster, 28
'Rosemary Harkness', 46
'Roseraie de l'Haÿ', 39, *39*,
    40, *41*
'Rouleti', 70
'Royal William', 45, 48, *49*
rubus, 15
rugosa, 14, 17, 20, *21*
    'Alba', 17, *21*
Rugosa roses, 11, 33, 34, 36,
    39, *39*, 40

'Sadler's Wells', 36
'Sarah van Fleet', 36, 39
'Savoy Hotel', 46
'Scarlet Fire', 36–7
'Seagull', 65, 66, *67*
sericea subsp. *omeiensis* f.
    pteracantha, 17, 20, *21*
sericea pteracantha, 10
'Sexy Rexy', 53, 56, *57*
'Shine On', 71, 72
'Shocking Blue', 54
shrub roses, 10, 11, *11*, 14, 17–18,
    20, 23, 24, 25, 32–41, *64*
'Silver Jubilee', 46, 48, *49*
'Sir Cedric Morris', 65
'Sir Frederick Ashton', 37
'Souvenir de la Malmaison', 25

'Souvenir de la Malmaison,
    Climbing', 61
Species roses, 10, 12–21, 76, *76*
spider plants, *11*
'Stacey Sue', 70
standards, 11, *28*, 35, 37, 38, *39*,
    40, 48, 52, 55, 56, 61, 72, 74,
    75, 77
'Starina', 70, *70*
'Stars 'n' Stripes', 70, 72
'Sunset Boulevard', 54
'Sunset Celebration', 46
'Swan Lake', 62, *62*
sweet briar, 17
'Sweet Dream', *70*, 71, 72, *73*

Taxus, 8
Tea roses, 6–7, 24, 29, 44
'Tequila Sunrise', 47, *47*, 48, *49*
'The Garland', 65
'The Times Rose', 52
'Top Marks', 71, 72, *73*
'Tour de Malakoff', 26
Tree roses, 24
'Trumpeter', 52, *52*, 56, *57*
'Tuscany', 28

'Vanity', 38
'Variegata di Bologna', 25
'Versicolor', 28, *28*
villosa, 17
Viola:
    V. cornuta, 55
    V. tricolor 'Bowles Black', 55
virginiana, 17

'Warm Welcome', 71
'Warm Wishes', 11, 46
webbiana, 18
'Wedding Day', *64*, 65
'Whisky Mac', 46, 48, *49*
'White Cockade', 62
wichurana, 14, 15–16, *15*, 20
Wild Roses, 10, 14
'Wilhelm', 38
'William Lobb', 29, 30, *31*
willmottiae, 18

'Zéphirine Drouhin', 61, *61*,
    66, *67*

Picture credits

The publishers would like to thank the photographers and garden owners for allowing us to reproduce the photographs on the following pages:

Endpapers: M. Harpur/Royal National Rose Society, St. Albans, Herts; 1 Micky White/Garden Picture Library; 2 J. Harpur/design: Arabella Lennox-Boyd; 3 Andrew Lawson; 4–5 Anne Hyde/design: Tessa King-Farlow, Birmingham; 6 top M. Harpur; 6 below J. Harpur/Hazelby House, Newbury, Berks; 7 top left Anne Hyde/Helen Faulls, London; 7 below left Anne Hyde/Lower Severalls, Somerset; 7 centre right J. Harpur/The Dower House, Castle Hedingham, Essex; 8–9 J. Harpur/Saling Hall, Essex; 10 Anne Hyde/Judy Brown, Masham Manor, Surrey; 10–11 J. Harpur/Parc Bagatelle, Paris, France; 11 Anne Hyde/Brendan Byrne, London; 12 J. Harpur; 13 J. Harpur/Beth Chatto Garden, Essex; 14 Clive Nichols/ Lower Hall, Shropshire; 14–15 above J. Harpur/Old Rectory, Sudborough, Northants; 14–15 below Didier Willery/Garden Picture Library; 16 J. Harpur/ Garsington Manor, Oxfordshire; 16–17 J. Harpur/Manor Farm, Birlington, Worcs; 17 Anne Hyde; 18 Andrew Lawson; 18–19 J. Harpur/Beth Chatto Garden, Essex; 20 Andrew Lawson; 21 clockwise from top left: J. Harpur/Royal National Rose Society, St. Albans, Herts; J. Harpur; J. Harpur/ Holker Hall, Cark-in-Cartmel, Cumbria; J. Glover/Garden Picture Library/ Mannington Hall, Norfolk; Anne Hyde; Andrew Lawson; 22 M. Harpur/Royal National Rose Society, St. Albans, Herts; 23 Clive Nichols; 24 Andrew Lawson; 24–25 J. Harpur/design: Tessa King-Farlow, Birmingham; 25 J. Harpur; 26 Anne Hyde/Sue Hillwood-Harris, London; 27 Clive Nichols/design: Wendy Lauderdale; 28 Andrew Lawson;

29 J. Harpur/design: Tessa Hobbs, Kirby Cane, Norfolk; 30 M. Harpur/Royal National Rose Society, St. Albans, Herts; 31 clockwise from top left: Justyn Willsmore/Sir Harold Hillier Gardens & Arboretum; Andrew Lawson; Clive Nichols; J. Harpur/House of Pitmuies, Angus, Scotland; Andrew Lawson; Andrew Lawson; Andrew Lawson; Clive Nichols; 32 J. Harpur/design: Tessa King-Farlow, Birmingham; 33 J. Harpur/ Park Farm, Chelmsford, Essex; 34 M. Harpur/ Sheila Chapman, Chelmsford, Essex; 34–35 Andrew Lawson; 36 left J. Harpur/ J. Scarman/Cottage Garden Roses; 36 right J. Harpur/Lower Hall, Shropshire; 37 J. Harpur; 38 J. Harpur/Park Farm, Chelmsford, Essex; 39 left J. Harpur/Gunilla Pickard, Fanners Green, Essex; 39 right Andrew Lawson; 40 Andrew Lawson; 41 clockwise from top left: J. Harpur; J. Harpur/ Royal National Rose Society, St. Albans, Herts; M. Harpur; Andrew Lawson; J. Harpur/ Royal National Rose Society, St. Albans, Herts; J. Harpur/Royal National Rose Society, St. Albans, Herts; J. Harpur; Andrew Lawson; 42 J. Harpur; 43 Mayer/Le Scanff/Garden Picture Library; 44 J. Harpur/ Nancy Schibanoff, Del Mar, CA, USA; 45 left Anne Hyde/Royal National Rose Society, St. Albans, Herts; 45 right Anne Hyde/Royal National Rose Society, St. Albans, Herts; 46 left David Askham/Garden Picture Library; 46 right David Askham/Garden Picture Library/Lackham College, Wiltshire; 47 left David Askham/Garden Picture Library; 47 right Lamontagne/ Garden Picture Library; 48 Andrew Lawson; 49 clockwise from top left: J. Harpur; Andrew Lawson; Brian Carter/ Garden Picture Library; J. Harpur/Royal National Rose Society, St. Albans, Herts; J. Glover/Garden Picture Library; Nick Wiseman/ A–Z Botanical; David Askham/Garden Picture Library; 50 Anne Hyde/

Royal National Rose Society, St. Albans, Herts; 51 J. Harpur/Sheila Chapman, Chelmsford, Essex; 52 left: J. S. Sira/Garden Picture Library; 52 right Andrew Lawson; 53 left J. Pavia/Garden Picture Library; 53 right Anne Hyde/Royal National Rose Society, St. Albans, Herts; 54 Brian Carter/Garden Picture Library; 54–55 M. Harpur/ Royal National Rose Society, St. Albans, Herts; 56 J. Harpur; 57 clockwise from top left: Dennis Davis/Garden Picture Library; J. Pavia/ Garden Picture Library; Jane Legate/ Garden Picture Library; J. Harpur; Micky White/Garden Picture Library; 58 J. Harpur/Deborah Kellaway, Bressingham, Norfolk; 59 M. Harpur; 60 top Anne Hyde/Ben Loftus, London; 60 centre M. Harpur/Old Rectory, Sudborough, Northants; 60 below J. Harpur/design: Mirabel Osler, Ludlow, Shropshire; 61 left J. Harpur; 61 right J. Harpur; 62 top J. Harpur/ Park Farm, Chelmsford, Essex; 62 below Andrew Lawson; 63 top J. Harpur; 63 below Andrew Lawson/Lime Kiln Rosarium, Suffolk; 64 left M. Harpur/ Kypp Cottage, Kent; 64 right Heather Angel; 65 M. Harpur/Kypp Cottage, Kent; 66 J. Harpur; 67 clockwise from top left: J. Harpur; Andrew Lawson; M. Harpur; Andrew Lawson; J. Harpur/Royal National Rose Society, St. Albans, Herts; J. Harpur/Royal National Rose Society, St. Albans, Herts; J. Harpur/Royal National Rose Society, St. Albans, Herts; Jo Whitworth; 68 J. Glover/Garden Picture Library/Help the Aged, Chelsea Flower Show; 69 J. S. Sira/Garden Picture Library; 70 J. Pavia/Garden Picture Library; 71 left J. S. Sira/Garden Picture Library; 71 right J. Glover/Garden Picture Library; 72 J. Harpur; 73 clockwise from top left: Andrew Lawson; H. Rice/Garden Picture Library; Andrew Lawson; Laslo Puskas/Garden Picture Library; Andrew Lawson; 80 J. Harpur.